T0287029

Praise for *Social Justice for the Sensitive Soul*

"Entering into activism can feel imperative but daunting, especially for those of us who are introverts or shy. Cheng-Tozun proposes a quieter, but no less impactful, approach: her gentle guidance urges us to get curious about finding our way to quiet activism, allowing us all to join in the march toward making the world a brighter place. A soulful book."

—Karen Walrond, author of *The Lightmaker's Manifesto* and *Radiant Rebellion*

"I wish this book existed earlier in my career, as it would've saved me so much struggle and stress! I'm so grateful for Dorcas Cheng-Tozun's voice, and her boldness in sharing her struggles and wisdom with us so that we know we're not alone as sensitive souls. We can make a unique difference in the world! The reflection questions after each chapter are also incredible and powerful journaling prompts that make this book priceless as a guide on our journeys."

—Grace Chiang Nicolette, vice president of Programming and External Relations, Center for Effective Philanthropy

"If you identify as an introvert, highly sensitive person, or empath you need *Social Justice for the Sensitive Soul* by Dorcas Cheng-Tozun to learn how to best bring your strengths, talents, and sense of purpose to social justice causes that are near and dear to your heart."

—Christine Rose Elle, author of *The Happy Empath* and *Daily Affirmations for Women*

"Upon simply reading the title, my soul sighed with relief. As I read these pages, I felt seen! I felt known! I felt celebrated! Dorcas Cheng-Tozun's words flow like the Holy Spirit whispering affirmation, encouragement, and appreciation for our intentional design—our quiet, potent strength, informed by prophetic foresight, as we reach for what is possible. She fosters freedom for the sensitive soul to just be and allow Spirit to create in and through us. This book is an important read as we learn to recognize and make room for the diversity of contributions that actually sustain justice work."

—Lucretia Carter Berry, PhD, president, Brownicity.com

"*Social Justice for the Sensitive Soul* is the first book I have read that fully embraces what so many of us who are Sensitives feel: a need to serve the greater good of humanity but to do so in ways that avoid burnout, compassion-fatigue, and apathy. Dorcas Cheng-Tozun gifts Sensitives with an incredible framework to understand and practice advocacy and activism on scales that reflect personal authenticity, sustainability, and optimal use of our time and energy while creatively and effectively contributing our often-prodigious empathy, conscientiousness, and heart-centered leadership."

—Tracy Cooper, PhD, author of *Thrive: The Highly Sensitive Person and Career*

"Writing with empathy and winsome honesty on this timely topic, Cheng-Tozun offers key insights relevant for *all* social changemakers. Her lived experience as a sensitive activist—along with the vivid stories of many others—provides a hopeful path forward for those who want to engage sustainably and authentically in the work of justice."

—Jody Chang, Chief Operating and Portfolio Officer, Silicon Valley Social Venture Fund

"The work of justice is hard. Moving the needle on lasting social change requires a deep dive into who we are, where we are from, our values, and an understanding of the gifts we each bring to the world. Those gifted with sensitivity have incredible insights others do not, naturally set apart from the status quo of ego-centered engagements. Their heart-centered connection to people and places is what this present moment is desperately calling for. In *Social Justice for the Sensitive Soul*, writer Dorcas Cheng-Tozun takes you on an affirming journey of self-discovery and contemplative reflection on each person's unique place in pursuing change to create a world in which all can thrive."

—Byron Chung, executive director, Ignite Institute at the Pacific School of Religion

"This book is a thorough, inspiring, and empowering exploration of the topic of highly sensitive people and social justice activism. The author writes from a basis of well-grounded and informed understanding of what high sensitivity and social justice activism are, honoring the important gift of activism that HSPs in particular bring to the world—*especially when they do it their own way.*"

—Barbara Allen, founder, Growing Unlimited

"As an introverted and highly sensitive activist, I've struggled to find ways to be an effective campaigner using my talents without burning out. This is the first social change book I've read where I felt understood, valued, and supported. I'm so glad this book exists for us gentle protesters around the world! A thoughtful, poignant, and empowering book shining a spotlight on world-changing quiet ways to protest and improve our fragile world."

—Sarah P. Corbett, award-winning activist and author of *How to Be a Craftivist: The Art of Gentle Protest*

"If you've ever felt too sensitive or too fragile to join the work of social justice, this book is for you. While we sensitive and empathic folks might often perceive our sensitivity as a liability to our activism, Cheng-Tozun asserts that our sensitivity is, in fact, a gift to reformation movements, writing, 'The shortest path toward progress is built on nonviolence, empathy, and inclusion.' These are all gifts embodied naturally by deep feelers! *Social Justice for the Sensitive Soul* offers a playbook for quiet, effective social transformation, a panacea for nonprofit burnout, and a way to stay sane when the work of changing the world feels like *too much* for any of us."

—Liz Charlotte Grant, author of the Empathy List newsletter and host of the *Zealot* podcast

"Dorcas Cheng-Tozun has created a book for the rest of us: a book for those whose hearts are on the line and who need a different way forward when it comes to confronting injustice, oppression, and hatred. *Social Justice for the Sensitive Soul* has filled a void I didn't know existed, but if Gandhi can learn how to leverage his innate sensitivity for good, then maybe I can too."

—Cara Meredith, author of *The Color of Life*

"In *Social Justice for the Sensitive Soul*, Dorcas Cheng-Tozun offers a brilliant thesis and a timely message penned with the authenticity of lived experience. Part love-letter and part manifesto, it's a must-read for any and all empath changemakers who are called to social change work, but shun the limelight of activism or heropreneurship of social innovation. Savor this book and then pass it on."

—Anita Nowak, PhD, author of *Purposeful Empathy* and lecturer at McGill University

"*Social Justice for the Sensitive Soul* is a beautifully written book that addresses a topic of critical importance and relevance for highly sensitive people: how to truly and authentically make a difference in the world. This will surely inspire and empower sensitive individuals to be the change in their own unique and wonderful ways."

—Andre Sólo, founder of Sensitive Refuge and author of *Sensitive*

"Cheng-Tozun creates a spacious place for many types of folks in the social justice movement. This book expands and stirs the imagination for the types of people needed to lead and sustain social change. This book provides a particularly poignant case for the gifts that sensitive souls bring to social justice, but the book is applicable to leadership and education settings as well. A thoughtful, stirring, and deeply hopeful book."

—Nikki Toyama-Szeto, executive director of Christians for Social Action

"This is a work of tremendous, hard-won hope that will speak to every social justice activist, not just the empaths. Dorcas Cheng-Tozun is a wise and gentle guide offering real help to those who have found themselves crushed by the outsize expectations of other activists and movements. Justice is not an ideal to which we sacrifice ourselves and our well-being. Dorcas helps us chart a path toward healthy engagement that includes self-awareness, silence, solitude, and rest—leading not to burnout but to deeper resilience and purpose."

—Jim Martin, vice president of spiritual formation, International Justice Mission

"I am a highly sensitive person called to seek justice in the world, but sometimes I worry I'm not strong enough for this work because I feel things deeply. I worry I'm not smart or educated enough because I overthink, and I've worried I don't care enough when I'm prone to overwhelm that leads to paralysis. I wish I had *Social Justice for the Sensitive Soul* when I was first beginning in ministry. Through Dorcas's research, storytelling, and gentle care for her reader, I see that I am exactly the person the world needs me to be—highly sensitive and all. This is a book I will treasure and return to many times for encouragement and insight."

—Osheta Moore, pastor and author of *Shalom Sistas* and *Dear White Peacemakers*

"Dorcas Cheng-Tozun offers us a gift in *Social Justice for the Sensitive Soul,* providing a pathway for the deep feelers and high empaths among us to fully engage in the work of social justice as we are, without the need to become someone else. Those of us who feel everything deeply need a way of being that allows us to engage in justice-oriented work without the fear of burning out. The wisdom in this book provides just that."

—Drew Jackson, poet and author of *God Speaks through Wombs* and *Touch the Earth*

"If your heart is stirred by the injustices all around you, yet you also struggle to understand how to confront those injustices in a manner that aligns with who God created you to be, *Social Justice for the Sensitive Soul* is the resource you need. Dorcas Cheng-Tozun has created a gracious, life-giving book full of wisdom, stories, and insights to encourage and empower you in the work of justice. It is possible to care deeply about justice and also take care of your own sensitive soul; Dorcas's book is a wonderful guide to help you in the journey."

—Helen Lee, co-author of *The Race-Wise Family* and author of *The Missional Mom*

Social Justice
for the
Sensitive Soul

Social Justice *for the* Sensitive Soul

HOW TO CHANGE THE WORLD IN QUIET WAYS

Dorcas Cheng-Tozun

Broadleaf Books
Minneapolis

SOCIAL JUSTICE FOR THE SENSITIVE SOUL
How to Change the World in Quiet Ways

Cover design and Illustration by Faceout Studio, Amanda Hudson

Print ISBN: 978-1-5064-8343-6
eBook ISBN: 978-1-5064-8344-3

To Jonah and Isaac
May joy-filled purpose always find you

Contents

PART III: Pathways and Possibilities

Introduction

"In a gentle way, you can shake the world."

Mahatma Gandhi

In the late nineteenth century, a quiet, unassuming young man named Mohandas boarded a steamship to travel from his native India to England to study law. Being a lawyer hadn't been the eighteen-year-old's first choice, but his father had pressured him to pursue the profession. He decided to make the most of it, taking the chance to see another part of the world. But he struggled with culture shock from the moment he left his home country. On the steamship and after arriving in London, he was embarrassed by how differently he behaved and dressed. He just couldn't seem to find his place.

In search of people to connect with, he joined the London Vegetarian Society and was elected a member of the executive committee. The law student faithfully attended every meeting. But, try as he might, he couldn't bring himself to speak.

Everyone else seemed more articulate, more opinionated, and sharper in their thinking.

"But I was at a loss to know how to express myself. All the rest of the members appeared to me to be better informed than I," he reflected later. "Then it often happened that just when I had mustered up courage to speak, a fresh subject would be started. This went on for a long time."[1]

It wasn't that he didn't have anything to say. Mohandas had plenty of thoughts; he just couldn't quite put them together and verbalize them on the spot. He tried different ways of participating and sharing his views. He would write his thoughts down before meetings. Sometimes, if reading his own words felt too difficult, he asked someone else to read them for him. When he did speak, he was prone to anxiety and losing his train of thought. On occasion, his body shook and his vision blurred. In the Vegetarian Society and elsewhere, he avoided large crowds, resisted small talk, and never gave impromptu remarks.

Far later in life, this "constitutional shyness," as he called it, which had been a source of shame and embarrassment in his younger days, became a distinct advantage that would shake the world. "Its greatest benefit has been that it has taught me the economy of words," Mohandas said. "I have naturally formed the habit of restraining my thoughts. . . . It has allowed me to grow. It has helped me in my discernment of truth."[2]

Today, many would consider Mohandas's own descriptions of his "shyness" and introversion as evidence that he was highly sensitive.[3] A highly sensitive person (HSP), according to Dr. Elaine N. Aron, the clinical psychologist who discovered this personality type and coined the term, can be recognized by these four traits: depth of processing, quicker to overstimulation, emotional reactivity, and sensing the subtle.[4] Mohandas, the glossophobic of the London Vegetarian Society, needed longer than his colleagues to process his thoughts. He had an intense, visceral response to being the center of attention. He was highly attuned to any ridicule or impatience he might see in the eyes of his colleagues.

But rather than fighting who he was, over time Mohandas learned to embrace his innate sensitivity. To leverage it. To use it for good. And in so doing, he changed the world.

Mohandas Karamchand Gandhi, more commonly known as Mahatma Gandhi, is often considered the founder of the modern nonviolence movement, which has toppled oppressive systems and inspired peace across the globe. His work and writings stirred other prominent social justice leaders, including Dr. Martin Luther King Jr., Nelson Mandela, and Cesar Chavez, to advocate for change through some of the methods of civil disobedience and nonviolent resistance Gandhi employed.

Even as a leader, Gandhi was never a formidable figure. He remained soft-spoken throughout his remarkable life. Much of the revolutionary change he brought about stemmed from a series of simple but powerful acts of resistance: walking out of a courtroom that did not allow him to wear his turban, fasting, marching for twenty-four days, boycotting British-made products. He also spent long periods of time at his ashram in Ahmedabad, India, focused on prayer, fasting, meditation, and welcoming pilgrims.[5]

Gandhi could not have achieved and inspired all that he did without the gifts that typically accompany sensitivity: empathy, perception, study, observation, an innate connection to sadness, and an ability to bond with others at the core of who they are and what they need. His example demonstrates the incredible influence and power that highly sensitive people have to contribute to the social good.

He is an inspiration for many people, including those of us who also hate large crowds or public speaking. Or those of us who have admittedly irrational fears, like Gandhi's longstanding fear of the dark.[6]

While sensitive, empathic people can certainly bring about revolutionary social change, most of us won't follow the path of Gandhi. And that's perfectly fine. The world doesn't need a billion Gandhis. There are many other richly meaningful roles we can fill, and many more role models we can emulate.

As a highly sensitive person, I needed years—decades, in all honesty—before I understood that I didn't have to be anything like Gandhi to still contribute to social justice causes. I had to find my own path, to do it in my own way, based on my own passions, skills, and limitations. Of course, such wisdom could apply to anyone, but it is especially pertinent for highly sensitive and empathic people, who risk deep emotional wounds and permanent burnout if they do not act with self-awareness and intentionality, understanding their strengths and limits. Even Gandhi could only be Gandhi because he accepted the whole picture of who he was and spent long seasons in quiet and solitude discerning his identity and calling.

Fortunately, there are plenty of places and spaces for sensitive, empathic, quiet, and introverted change agents. We are collectively holding ourselves back if we fail to embrace the unique and wonderful gifts—talents, perspectives, ideas, approaches—that sensitive people have to offer.

With those gifts, sensitive people tend to go all in with social justice efforts—which inevitably puts our hearts on the line. As we do, we encounter historical forces, systemic forces, social forces, dogmatic forces, political forces, and individual forces that resist a more equitable distribution of rights, resources, power, and privilege. We will encounter anger and hatred, frustration and apathy, disgust and fear. There are many who would gladly throw down anchors to slow or stop our efforts.

And sometimes the pain originates much closer to home. Harmful words and actions may come even from collaborators, colleagues, or clients. Not everyone you try to serve, help, or partner with is going to appreciate you.

So, for sensitive individuals who want to join the fray but are susceptible to being deeply affected by what we encounter, how can we know what kind of work we should do? How do we know how much we can handle? And how can we advocate for good causes in a way that is not only sustainable but also allows us to live authentically and joyfully? Those are the questions at the core of this book, which offers support, resources, and ideas for your journey.

This book is for anyone interested in engaging with social justice who identifies as sensitive, empathic, quiet, introverted, or melancholic. Generally speaking, such individuals are typically part of three overlapping groups: the highly sensitive, the highly empathic, and the highly introverted. Individuals in all three of these categories tend to have complex inner lives, be creative, and connect deeply with others.

Each of these groups can also be identified by particular traits: Those who are highly sensitive have *sensory processing sensitivity*, or *high environmental sensitivity*, when both the nervous system and cognitive processes are triggered more easily and deeply by stimuli. They tend toward shifting emotions, anxiety, and being withdrawn, as well as an openness to experiences.[7] Dr. Aron estimates that up to 20 percent of the population are HSPs.[8]

Those who are highly empathic feel and absorb other people's emotions or physical symptoms or even intuit the energy of the surrounding environment. While many people may be empathic to some degree, recent research estimates that only 1–2 percent of the population can be considered highly empathic.[9]

Introverts, who make up as much as half of the population, are recognized by their enjoyment of and need for solitude.[10] Even introverts who enjoy being with other people need to balance that with time alone.

It's not uncommon to identify with more than one of these categories. Most empaths, for example, are also sensitive. Highly empathic people cannot move in the world without being deeply affected by the people and things around them, readily absorbing others' joy, sorrow, hope, and fear as their own. Some introverts may be considered sensitive, while others are not.[11] The *highly* introverted are far more likely to be easily overwhelmed by external stimuli, including crowds, noise, and conflict, just like the highly sensitive.[12]

Regardless of categories or definitions, as long as you identify with some of the traits described above, this book is for you. For the sake of simplicity, I primarily refer to such individuals as *sensitive* or *empathic*. These terms encompass many of the qualities—longer processors, deep feelers, easily overstimulated and overwhelmed—that can make justice work particularly challenging and risky.

Recent studies of serotonin- and dopamine-regulating genes have shown that sensitivity is predominantly innate.[13] We are simply born this way, preprogrammed and hard-wired to be more attuned to stimuli and to more deeply process them. While some of us may want to wish our sensitivity away, it's important to know that, even if we wanted to, we cannot bury it, ignore it, or train it away.

Sensitivity is actually a beautiful personality quality that promotes connection, compassion, creativity, and inclusion. As sensitive individuals, we often see what others cannot: the voice that's being unheard, the perspective that's been forgotten, the problem that hasn't been addressed, the unintended consequences that haven't been named.

Gandhi is only one of many deeply admired reformers whose emotional depth and empathy strengthened their leadership and influence. Abraham Lincoln, Mother Teresa, Martin Luther King Jr., and Jane Goodall also number among the sensitive.[14] And for every Mother Teresa, there are tens of thousands of other dedicated souls quietly changing their corner of the world in their own unique way. Sensitive people carry fiercely glowing flames that our world needs to burn away injustice, oppression, and hatred.

Sensitivity comes in as many flavors as there are people. How we experience and express our sensitivity is deeply affected by a variety of factors, including our childhoods, families of origin, culture, age, past traumas, levels of self-confidence and self-awareness, mental and physical health, and our many personality traits (aside from sensitivity) that make us each unique. While I'll be addressing characteristics and tendencies that apply to *most* sensitive individuals, it's possible that some things don't apply to you. That's fine. There will, hopefully, still be enough that resonates with you as you walk your own journey of social justice.

Let me also take a moment to explain what I mean by social justice work. One definition I've found helpful is from *The Dictionary of Environment and Conservation*, which calls *social justice* "the objective of creating a fair and equal society in which each individual matters, their rights are recognized and protected, and decisions are made in ways that are fair and honest."[15] The four essential goals of social justice are human rights, access, participation, and equality, though the pursuit of these goals could take many forms.[16]

For us sensitive individuals, that's excellent news. With so many possibilities, we are far more likely to discover meaningful and sustainable ways to contribute.

That doesn't mean finding our place will be easy. Being a sensitive soul in social justice work requires, to a large extent, the courage to be countercultural. It requires a deep self-awareness of what you can and cannot do. It requires focus and limits. It requires a careful consideration of people, situations, and environments. It requires an understanding that you cannot change all things or be all things to all people—but you can certainly make a meaningful difference.

Let me say a bit about how this book is organized. The first of three sections explores the particular gifts and limitations of being a sensitive individual and how we might discover our place in the broader context of social justice efforts. The second section explores the various considerations to weigh when trying to find the right niche. And the last section delves into specific areas of work where sensitive people, past and present, have thrived while doing tremendous good, which will hopefully provide inspiration for your own next steps.

Remember: you are *exactly* who the world needs you to be. Author Susan Cain, in her best sellers *Quiet: The Power of Introverts in a World That Can't Stop Talking* and *Bittersweet: How Sorrow and Longing Make Us Whole,* discusses the necessary and essential balance between different kinds of people in society. Introverts help temper extroverts, while melancholy souls harmonize meaningfully with their more buoyant peers. Each enhances and strengthens the other. Together, both are far more powerful.

Similarly, as sensitive people, we are a necessary balance to our less sensitive counterparts. We need one another to do more, to do better, and to do it more thoughtfully, comprehensively, and effectively. Together, we can accomplish far more in expanding access to dignity, opportunity, and equality to our fellow human beings.

Part I

The Sensitive Soul

1

The Gifts and Limitations of Sensitivity

"Highly sensitive beings suffer more but they also love harder, dream wider and experience deeper horizons and bliss."

Victoria Erickson

When I entered the nonprofit sector as a young professional, I often thought about social justice leaders like Gandhi. As a sophomore in college, I had participated in a weeklong service-learning trip that lit a fire in my belly for social justice. I wanted to dedicate my career to righting every wrong I encountered during my limited time on earth.

Somewhere along the way, I developed a clear picture in my mind of who I had to be in order to be an effective change agent. I wanted to be an unflinching advocate for the marginalized and suffering. I wanted to be an unceasing voice calling for change—loudly, compellingly, and articulately. I wanted to challenge powerful people, bring down unjust systems, and break cycles of poverty, violence, and corruption.

And while I was busy saving the world, I would also be the kind of person who'd happily sacrifice anything for a good cause. I would live anywhere without complaint. I would give anyone in need the shirt off my back, the food in my refrigerator, and the small savings in my bank account.

This view of who I thought I was—or who I *could* be if only I tried hard enough—was the major reason I moved to China when I was twenty-nine years old. The move required leaving my family, my friends, my job, my culture, most of my belongings, and the only home I had ever known. All I moved with were my spouse and two large suitcases.

But I gladly went because it was all for a good cause. My husband, Ned, had started a business, called d.light, to provide affordable, high-quality solar products to families without electricity in developing countries. He and his cofounders were manufacturing their products in Shenzhen, an industrial megacity in southern China; we were moving there to set up an operations office.

The cause was so good—we were potentially providing greater health, safety, and opportunity to *billions* of people—that I determined to do and be anything that was necessary. I could sacrifice anything. I could face any challenge. I was sure of it.

Ten months and many stressful experiences after our move, what seemed a minor misperception about myself nearly broke me. One day, I sat with Ned at a Public Security Bureau station in Shenzhen, where we had to register as foreign nationals on a quarterly basis. About an hour into our wait, as stern-faced individuals came and went in an endless bureaucratic assembly line, a thought suddenly materialized in my mind: *I can't do this anymore.* I began to see spots in front of me. My heart raced. Breathing, that most natural of activities, became strangely difficult.

I grabbed Ned's sleeve. "I don't feel good," I gasped.

He looked at me with alarm. After an assessing moment, he said, "Okay, just hang in there until we're done here."

My entire body remained clenched, my breathing uneven and labored as we finished our registration and took a taxi home. Once back in our twenty-second story flat within a nondescript, concrete high-rise, I collapsed on our couch and wept uncontrollably for the next four hours.

It was the worst and longest panic attack I had ever experienced. And it was only the beginning. For nearly a year after that, I did little more than sleep and cry and journal. Unable to work, I quit my job and rarely left our apartment. I filled at least three journals with tear-smudged questions that clawed at the very root of who I was: *Why did this happen? What is wrong with me? Why can't I handle what everyone else seems to be managing perfectly well?*

Like an ice shelf that suddenly collapses into the sea after years of unseen melting and fracturing, my breakdown had actually been a long time coming. I had spent years trying to be an idealized version of myself—working long hours, pushing myself in challenging roles, never saying no, and regularly placing myself in contexts that petrified me. When my body communicated stress, I ignored it; I didn't listen to my heart when it ached from pain, sorrow, and exhaustion. I had taken hold of all the traits I liked most about being sensitive, without paying attention to any of my limitations.

One of the most wonderful traits of sensitive individuals is that they tend to be very conscientious, caring deeply about the well-being of others. We are idealistic and hope for a better world. In a recent survey I conducted of 204 sensitive and empathic individuals, a whopping 96 percent said they felt a moderate or high sense of responsibility about social justice issues. When asked how much they stayed informed about social justice issues, 88 percent responded with either "a lot" or "some." And eight out of ten respondents had engaged in some form of social justice work, service, or activism. We are a compassionate, considerate, and motivated bunch.

Unsurprisingly, empathic people have a profound longing for meaningful activities and work.[1] We are so aware of the wrongs and the suffering around us that we can't help but want to make things better. We want to open our hearts and wallets, to use our hands and feet for social good.

But that longing is a double-edged sword, potentially pushing us into roles and responsibilities that take a huge toll on us. To be a sensitive person whose heart beats for social justice is to be perpetually pulled between two poles. On one side is our love for goodness and justice, for equity and inclusiveness. But drawing us in another direction is our more limited tolerance for stress and stimulation, our tendency toward melancholy. We are weighed down far more by what we absorb from the people and environments around us, including the hardship and suffering we meet. Many things can begin to feel like just too much: too much stress, too much noise, too much pressure, too much pain, too much conflict.

And in the work of social justice, the stakes couldn't be higher; the outcome couldn't be more important; the opposing forces couldn't be more entrenched.

We sensitives are aware of all this—intuitively, emotionally, physically, and intellectually. We carry the burden of pushing for social change in our muscles and veins. Our brains are easily flooded with norepinephrine and cortisol when under stress.[2] Our expansive hearts collect the anger, frustration, despair, sorrow, and grief that is infused throughout social justice work. And our neurons fire as we ruminate—again and again, over long periods of time—about society's ills, possible solutions, our contributions, our mistakes, and how we can do better. These elements all make for an incredibly intense inner world that, if we allow it to, can churn within us every moment of every day. Add to that a social justice-related job, volunteer role, or moonlighting gig full of passion, hardship, and stress—a very intense external world—and you can see why the risk of burnout, exhaustion, depression, and anxiety would be extraordinarily high.

In the nonprofit sector in the United States, there's already a burnout epidemic. According to a survey by organizational development consulting firm Opportunity Knocks, as many as half of nonprofit employees are burned out or on the verge of burnout.[3] A separate survey by Nonprofit HR found that 45 percent of nonprofit employees were planning to look for a different job in the next year, with nearly a quarter of those individuals looking to leave the nonprofit sector altogether.[4]

In the survey I conducted, about six out of ten respondents said that they had burned out while engaged in social justice work. Among those, over 90 percent had burned out multiple times, with nearly one-third saying that they had burned out *five or more times.*

Burnout, a term first coined in 1975 by pioneering psychologist Herbert Freudenberger, has what he describes as three primary components: emotional exhaustion, depersonalization through a depletion of empathy and caring, and a sense of futility, or the idea that nothing you do can make a difference.[5]

For sensitive individuals, burning out can feel like a disintegration of some of the most fundamental aspects of your identity, including your idealism, your emotional energy, and your deep connection to other people. It is disorienting and distressing. A serious episode of burnout may require months or years to recover from. If significant enough, burnout can be a form of trauma, which, according to psychiatrist and trauma researcher Bessel van der Kolk, "produces actual physiological changes, including a recalibration of the brain's alarm system, an increase in stress hormone activity, and alterations in the system that filters relevant information from irrelevant. We now know that trauma compromises the brain area that communicates the physical, embodied feeling of being alive."[6] To experience burnout is to harm your mind and body in serious ways.

I am among those multiple-burnout survivors. My experience in China, while particularly dramatic, was only one of several times that I emotionally crashed and burned and had to quit my job. Those traumatic experiences fundamentally altered my mental and physical health, each time lowering my tolerance for stress. Even now, after a couple decades of exploring, pivoting, and experimenting with multiple roles, organizations, and industries, I feel like burnout constantly lurks just around the bend, waiting to sweep my legs out from under me.

Sometimes I shake my fists at the heavens and demand to know why I care so deeply about contributing to social change, yet I don't seem to have the right personality traits for the job. Along with substantial sensitivities, I have chronic anxiety. The traumas of losing my father at a young age, spiritual abuse, and race- and gender-based harassment have affected me deeply. I *feel* things—my own emotions and those I absorb from others—with such intensity that they frequently overwhelm me. Stress, uncertainty, or difficult people easily deplete me.

Your experiences, stress tolerance, or sensitivity levels may be different, but for many of us who are sensitive, we often feel miles away from the profile of the social change agent we'd like to be. Where is the fearlessness, the endless drive and energy, the conviction and clarity that so many others have? How can we hope to effect systemic transformation when we have so many emotional and physical limitations?

I often think of climate change activist Greta Thunberg, who, with an assist from her Asperger's syndrome, stubbornly and persistently faces down some of the world's most powerful leaders and remains singularly focused on saving our planet.[7] Or education activist Malala Yousafzai, who famously said in a 2009 television interview, "All I want is an education. And I am afraid of no one."[8] Three years later, at the age of fifteen, she was shot in the head by the Taliban. After recovering, she continued her advocacy on an even bigger world stage. As young adults, Thunberg and Yousafzai have demonstrated a courage rivaling that of the most valiant warriors.

The sphere of social justice—with its activism and advocacy, protests and pushback, debates and callouts—does not seem like the right place for tenderhearted, easily overwhelmed individuals. But it's exactly where we need to be. Humanity needs our conscientious, intuitive, creative, compassionate souls at the forefront of addressing our most painful and pressing challenges. Renowned psychologist Carl Jung, likely a highly sensitive person himself, considered sensitive individuals as "educators and promoters of culture" with particular access to "prophetic foresight" and the ability to teach "the other possibility."[9]

Taking the risk to enter into meaningful but stretching activities can also be good for our own development and character. The more we engage with other people and environments, the more we strengthen our ability to tolerate stimulation. It can be a slow process, but we may even grow to appreciate and enjoy the activities and stimuli that previously overwhelmed us. "The way to come to tolerate and then enjoy being involved in the world," says Dr. Aron, "is by being in the world."[10]

To do this in a sustainable, authentic way, though, requires us to direct our deep thinking toward understanding our own skills, interests, and limitations. It requires us to apply our creativity toward figuring out where we fit in the mosaic of social change efforts. It requires our breaking the aspirational mold of trying to be just like Gandhi or Greta Thunberg or Malala Yousafzai. Even more so, it requires extending our wide and robust compassion toward ourselves and listening carefully to the warning signals of our hearts, minds, and bodies. We contribute the most when we contribute from a healthy place, living out the reality that we are but one individual among many working together for the social good.

Maybe you won't be the one holding the megaphone at a protest or demanding justice at a press conference. Perhaps you'd rather not march through the offices of elected officials or argue in federal court on behalf of disenfranchised groups. You may not have the capacity to relocate overseas or move into the slums. You may not want to phone bank or do door-to-door canvassing. Don't be discouraged. There are plenty of caring, talented people who are not highly sensitive or highly empathic who can fill those roles.

In the past century, the greatest, most impactful social movements have been made up of all kinds of people doing all kinds of different activities. There have been writers and philosophers, artists and administrators, engineers and scientists, teachers and historians, secretaries and accountants. Social change has come about through kindness, friendship, data, technology, art, ideas, research, mentorship, dialogue, and more. No matter your particular flavor of sensitivity, there is a place for you to contribute in a unique and meaningful way.

Yes, stepping into the arena of social justice can be frightening and confusing. There will be challenges without clear answers; there will be hard experiences and intimidating people. The role that best fits you will probably change and evolve as you change and evolve.

But if you feel that pounding in your heart or that fire in your gut that wants to make a meaningful difference in the world, I hope you'll listen to it. The world is desperately in need of more sensitive people to join the movement for change.

Reflection Questions

1. In the past, what type of social activist have you tried to be? How has that fit with your personality and your particular strengths and limitations?
2. In the push and pull between wanting to advocate for social justice and needing to honor your sensitivities and needs, which direction have you gone in most frequently? How has this affected you?

3. What social justice-related activities have been the most challenging for you? How might that have been connected to your sensitive, empathic, or introverted nature?
4. Do you have particular traits and characteristics that seem to get in the way of doing social justice work? How could you turn this self-criticism into self-compassion?

2

Why the World Needs You

"The real warriors in this world are the ones
that see the details of another's soul."

Shannon L. Alder

In the Indo-European cultures of old, there were generally two types of leaders: warrior kings and priestly advisers. The warrior kings, as you might expect, preferred aggression and quick, decisive action. They prioritized freedom and expansion and fame. Warrior kings almost always wanted more—more resources, more land, more people, more control—without necessarily considering the long-term consequences of their desires.[1]

But societies didn't survive long if led only by warrior kings; communities also needed thoughtful, compassionate, creative, and wise priestly advisers. Priestly advisers would observe, listen, consider, gather, plan, and generate. They provided an important check on and counterbalance to the warrior kings, encouraging inclusionary decision-making and thoughtful action. Throughout history, when both of these archetypal styles of leadership were present, societies were more balanced, healthy, and inclusive.

In today's world, the highly sensitive person operates much like the ancient priestly advisers, explains Dr. Elaine Aron in her book *The Highly Sensitive Person*. In every generation, humanity has needed people who consistently point to the North Star, lean heavily on wisdom, and empower the entire community to flourish. "You," Aron writes, addressing her highly sensitive readers, "were born to be among the advisors and thinkers, the spiritual and moral leaders of your society."[2]

Sensitive people can fill this role because we are intuitive and meticulous, seeing and recognizing things that most others don't. We understand people well and often can see both sides of an issue. We're able to sense when a plan is problematic, when someone can't be trusted, when unintended consequences will cause great harm. We take the necessary time to process and then process again, considering past events as well as future possibilities. We are often excellent students of history and careful architects of the future.

But we can also be overlooked. Many societies, particularly Western societies in North America and Europe, lavish praise on warrior-king types. In these societies, aggression and outspokenness are respected and rewarded in nearly every sphere of life: business, academics, politics, sports, religion, and more. Those who speak louder, faster, and more often are considered stronger leaders and more knowledgeable experts.[3] Our societies place trust in those who act with self-confidence and assertiveness. We don't need to look any further than the ongoing popularity of authoritarian leaders like Vladimir Putin, Recip Erdogan, and Donald Trump in their respective countries to see this dynamic at play.

The world of social justice is no exception. Warrior-king personalities dominate public discourse and debate about social issues. The push toward social progress can, at times, feel like a combat field, as protesters and counterprotesters, police and activists battle each other in the streets. Hackers, doxxers, trolls, and influencers exchange digital fire—causing real-life damage through verbal abuse, bullying, privacy compromises, and threats to livelihood and physical safety. Even those whose views are on the right side of history may choose to engage in hostile, combative tactics in hopes of forcing change.

This skewing toward animosity, mistrust, and pugnacity is only getting worse around the globe. Experts warn that we have entered what they call an "age of anger," when shocking acts of mass violence, belligerent nationalism, hate groups, abuses of power, racism, sexism, xenophobia, homophobia, and more harm our communities and crowd our headlines and social media feeds on a regular basis.[4]

"The conflicts, not confined to fixed battlefields, feel endemic and uncontrollable. Hate-mongering against immigrants and minorities has gone mainstream; figures foaming at the mouth with loathing and malice are ubiquitous on old and new media alike," writes Indian-British author and journalist Panjak Mithra. He says the vast majority of people today feel entitled to their *own* individual freedom and prosperity, without regard for the damage this may cause to others.[5]

In concert with this trend, or perhaps in response to it, anger has become a key fuel for social justice movements and organizations. Yes, there is much to be angry about, and rightly so. Anger can be a powerful emotion spurring us to alter our behaviors or take action. In a study of anger in social activism, based on in-depth interviews with current and former employees of Amnesty International, one participant explained, "Anger is why we're all here, it's why we all chose to work in an NGO rather than somewhere else . . . anger at injustice . . . and even anger that we live the life we live."[6]

Anger gets things done. But warrior anger without priestly counsel can be a stunningly blunt instrument, often uncontrolled and causing plenty of collateral damage. When we are angry at the systems and structures, laws and precedents that perpetuate inequities and injustice, it becomes too easy to direct that anger toward individuals and groups we consider to be "on the other side." We may even turn our anger on allies who we see as failing to do what they should or direct anger toward ourselves for not doing more.

In fighting for what we consider to be right, we can too easily lose sight of what is good. In our desire to advocate for what is just, we may inadvertently disregard what is loving.

While anger has grown in our societies, empathy is on the decline. One study of American college students over three decades compared their responses to statements measuring empathy, such as "I often have tender, concerned feelings for people less fortunate than me."[7] From 1979 to 2009, the level of empathic concern declined by an alarming 48 percent, with the steepest rate of decline coming after 2000. Now, the average college student feels less empathy than three-quarters of college students surveyed in 1979. Researchers are still trying to determine the causes of this sharp downturn; among the possibilities are the rise of digital relationships and interactions, increased social isolation, and greater pressure on young people to achieve.[8] What remains clear is that "empathy seems to be endangered," neuroscientist Jamil Zaki of Stanford University claims.[9]

With less empathy, we are far more prone to regard people as the other, the different, or the enemy—something we see happening across the political spectrum. Conservatives accuse progressives of being too coddling, dependent, elitist, and politically correct. Progressives decry conservatives for being too ignorant, bigoted, privileged, and fragile. Anyone who has witnessed the last few American election cycles has seen the ugliness on full display. "We are sort of at the stage of polarization where there are more and more people who are seeking confrontation, where they are not simply satisfied with disagreeing with the other side or yelling at the other side, but they want to confront," said Mark Pitcavage, historian and senior research fellow at the Anti-Defamation League's Center on Extremism, in a *Washington Post* article. "We are not just a polarized society—we are increasingly a confrontational society now."[10]

It's clear that our current trajectory of animosity is not sustainable. Anger, conflict, and violence, even in the name of a sympathetic cause, inevitably beget more anger, conflict, and violence. Confrontation and aggression create more pain and grievances rather than the conversation and collaboration we need.

On an individual level, feeling perpetual anger increases our stress and anxiety, damaging our mental and physical health.[11] It strains our relationships. It pulls us toward more destructive behavior. There is the very real risk that anger run amok may cause great harm to ourselves, one another, and our planet.

Despite the ways societies revere the warrior king, relying on anger is actually *not* an effective strategy for social progress. We can see how this plays out in our efforts to influence the people around us. Humans are complex, stubborn creatures; our ideas and attitudes are determined by far more than reason. This has been proven over decades of social psychology research that consistently demonstrate the behaviors we rely on to protect ourselves and our beliefs. *Confirmation bias*, for example, is our tendency to cherry-pick only the information that supports what we already believe and disregard any information that challenges our beliefs. *Myside bias*, coined by cognitive scientists Hugo Mercier and Dan Sperber, refers to our ability to find weaknesses in someone else's argument while remaining happily blind to shortcomings in our own position.[12] And the *boomerang effect* names the very real phenomenon that occurs when a message intended to positively influence fails to lead to change and can actually "backfire and cause an increase in the unhealthy or anti-social attitude or behavior targeted for change."[13] Trying to debate, argue, bully, or shame someone into changing their minds or admitting their wrongs is like asking a blue whale to fly. It simply doesn't work. When individuals on the other side of the argument have not been heard, understood, and respected, they are likely to walk away unchanged or even more entrenched in their beliefs and behaviors.

In a comprehensive study of 323 protest campaigns over the last century from around the world, Harvard University political scientist Erica Chenoweth discovered that nonviolent campaigns were twice as likely as violent campaigns to achieve their goals. Chenoweth and her colleague, Maria Stephen of the International Center of Nonviolent Conflict, focused primarily on attempts to bring about regime change from 1900 to 2006. They categorized movements as nonviolent only when they caused no known physical harm to people or property. Even with such a strict definition of what constituted nonviolent movements, they deduced that nonviolent campaigns had a 53 percent success rate, as compared to 26 percent for violent campaigns.

Chenoweth and Stephen also discovered that in order to secure major political change, at least 3.5 percent of the population must actively participate in protests. At this level of participation, everyday functions of society are so disrupted that change is necessitated. And this, in part, helps explain the success of nonviolent movements. They are more attractive and accessible to a larger proportion of the general population, which in turn increases the possibility that a campaign can reach the necessary participation rate for success.[14]

In big and small ways, the shortest path toward social progress is built on nonviolence, empathy, and inclusion. It is wide and welcoming, peaceful and loving. It seeks to see others, no matter where they stand on an issue, as fellow human beings first.

And who better to blaze those trails than those who embody these characteristics most fully—the sensitive and empathic, or the priestly advisers, among us?

The call for a more compassionate and gentle way to advocate for change is certainly not new. The ability to sincerely and effectively reach out to the opposition was one of Mahatma Gandhi's most remarkable qualities. "He never stood on ceremony, or hectored his opponents, no matter how far apart he stood from them on the issues at hand, whether he was addressing the king or a minor Raj official," writes biographer Roderick Matthews. "His ability to reach out informally across political and social divides was extraordinary."[15]

Martin Luther King Jr. admired Gandhi's commitment to befriending his enemies so much that he made that a central tenet of his own approach to nonviolence. According to the King Center, founded by Coretta Scott King to advance Dr. King's legacy of nonviolence, a cornerstone of his beliefs included this: "Nonviolence seeks friendship and understanding with the opponent. Nonviolence does not seek to defeat the opponent. Nonviolence is directed against evil systems, forces, oppressive policies, unjust acts, but not against persons. Through reasoned compromise, both sides resolve the injustice with a plan of action."[16]

Take Dr. King's famed "Letter from a Birmingham Jail," written in response to moderate white clergymen who had published an open letter critical of King. His letter is direct and strongly worded. But it is never disrespectful. In the opening paragraph, King says, "But since I feel that you are men of genuine good will and your criticisms are sincerely set forth, I would like to answer your statement in what I hope will be patient and reasonable terms." And after clearly and comprehensively deconstructing each of their arguments and making a powerful case for urgent, ongoing nonviolent action, King concludes, "If I have said anything in this letter that is an overstatement of the truth and is indicative of an unreasonable impatience, I beg you to forgive me. . . . I also hope that circumstances will soon make it possible for me to meet each of you, not as an integrationist or a civil rights leader, but as a fellow clergyman and a Christian brother."[17] Only with such an empathic approach do we have any hope of moving toward King's vision of "the beloved community," where our interactions with one another—whether or not we are in agreement—are based on love, nonviolence, inclusion, and trust.[18]

When we consider specific social justice causes, King's and Gandhi's leadership teaches us our ultimate aim should be higher and broader than winning an argument or passing legislation or removing a foe from power. We should, as much as possible, conduct our actions in hopes that genuine affection, collaboration, respect, and trust on a broad scale are possible.

At a 1960 press conference, King explained that "resistance and nonviolence are not in themselves good. There is another element that must be present in our struggle that then makes our resistance and nonviolence truly meaningful. That element is reconciliation. Our ultimate end must be the creation of the beloved community. The tactics of nonviolence without the spirit of nonviolence may indeed become a new kind of violence."[19] To call out, shame, belittle, cancel, or shout down those who think differently from us with the desire to win is to reject the spirit of nonviolence—making the formation of a beloved community that much harder.

A growing chorus of thought leaders and activists are now calling us once again to consider the way of Gandhi and King. In recent years, Black activist and writer adrienne maree brown has advocated for what she calls emergent strategy, based on the understanding that complex systems and patterns come out of, and can be changed by, a large number of relatively simple interactions. "In the framework of emergence, the whole is a mirror of the parts. Existence is fractal—the health of the cell is the health of the species and the planet," she explains.[20] Through this lens, every individual relationship matters. Every interaction matters, something that the wise priestly advisers understand well. "I can see the miraculous in others—even those who hate me have heartbeats, and, I generally assume, have people they love," she writes.[21]

Entrepreneur Chloé Valdary also advocates for a gentler approach to social change. Her Theory of Enchantment is a social and emotional learning program promoting authentic diversity and inclusion in schools, workplaces, and other environments. The three primary principles of the Theory of Enchantment may resonate if you identify as sensitive or empathic: (1) treat people like human beings, not political abstractions; (2) criticize to uplift and empower, never to tear down, never to destroy; and (3) root everything you do in love and compassion.[22] If this sounds familiar, it should. Valdary draws liberally from the teachings of Martin Luther King.

But as attractive as it may sound to go the way of kindness and compassion toward a more just and equal society, actually doing so is an extraordinarily hard road. There aren't masses of people lining up to learn and practice the tenets of conscientious, thoughtful nonviolence and reconciliation. Why? Because it is far easier to push for power, get angry, call out your enemies, and fight.

This, however, is precisely where sensitive individuals are particularly gifted. We are already advantaged with greater empathy; it is our preference to be kind and gentle with others rather than antagonistic. In many important ways, we hold the antidote to the age of anger—as long as we have the self-awareness, confidence, and courage to engage as who we truly are.

Reflection Questions

1. Can you think of examples of leaders you know who operate as warrior kings? How about leaders who are priestly advisers? What are the main differences between them and how they are received by others?

2. How have you seen the dominance of anger and the decline of empathy in your social justice work, your community, or online?
3. If our collective goals were for social change as well as the building up of "the beloved community," how would that change our approaches to activism?
4. Are there specific ways that you could consider taking a gentler, more kind and compassionate approach to social justice work?

3

Shedding the Activist Ideal

"To free us from the expectations of others,
to give us back to ourselves—there lies the
great, singular power of self-respect."
Joan Didion

"I wish I could be out there marching with you."

Nichelle Nichols, known for her groundbreaking role as communications officer Nyota Uhura on the original *Star Trek*, spoke those words in 1967 to Martin Luther King when she met him at a NAACP fundraiser after the show's first season. Her lament likely echoed that of many African Americans who couldn't join the civil rights marches happening in the South—perhaps due to work or financial constraints, the inability to travel, health issues, or the real threat of physical harm.

Maybe you have thought the same thing or even spoken it aloud. I know I have. I've seen protests and sit-ins and press conferences and advocacy campaigns on the news or social media, and I've wanted—desperately—to be there.

But, at the same time, as a sensitive person, I also *haven't* wanted to be there. The thought of participating in such loud, aggressive, contentious, risky social action terrifies me. I don't feel like I have it in me to do that and still manage my day-to-day responsibilities of working and taking care of my kids. In all likelihood, the resulting stress and trauma would probably outweigh any good resulting from my individual participation. Yet the thought persists: I should be there. I should at least *want* to be there.

At that NAACP dinner, I imagine Nichelle Nichols expected Dr. King to say she should join them on the streets when she could. Or she could use her growing fame to speak out more for civil rights. Those are the kinds of responses I've heard from friends and colleagues in social justice when I've sheepishly declined their invitations to go "out there."

Instead, according to an account Nichols shared with NPR in 2011, Dr. King responded: "No, no, no. No, you don't understand. We don't need you to march. You are marching. You are reflecting what we are fighting for. . . . For the first time, we are being seen the world over as we should be seen."

Dr. King went on to say that *Star Trek* was the only show he and his wife allowed their children to stay up late watching. And they watched because of Nichols—one of the only Black women on television portraying a strong and brilliant leader highly respected by all her colleagues, whether they were white men or aliens from a distant planet.[1]

Dr. King's response stunned the actress—and altered the trajectory of her life. Nichols had been planning to leave the show after its first season, leveraging her newfound recognition to pursue a different career path. Instead, after this exchange, she decided to stay on as Lieutenant Uhura. She ended up starring in seventy episodes of the *Star Trek* series and six *Star Trek* films, influencing an entire generation of Americans, especially Black Americans.[2] Her role included one of the first interracial kisses (between Lieutenant Uhura and Captain Kirk) on scripted US television. It aired just over a year after the US Supreme Court struck down state laws banning interracial marriage in the 1967 case *Loving v. Virginia*.[3]

In addition, Nichols's fictional role as a space traveler actually gave her influence over real-life space travel. After the original *Star Trek* series ended, Nichols volunteered with NASA to recruit more diverse astronauts, focusing on women and African Americans. She helped recruit Sally Ride and Guion Bluford, the first American female astronaut and Black astronaut, respectively.[4] The character of Lieutenant Uhura also inspired the lives and careers of Mae Jemison, the first African American woman in space; Whoopi Goldberg, who had a starring role in *Star Trek: The Next Generation*; Barack Obama, the first Black president of the United States; and countless others.[5]

Nichelle Nichols's work as an actress, which at first glance might seem inconsequential compared to the efforts of those marching, sitting at lunch counters, and registering voters, actually contributed meaningfully to the civil rights movement and social progress on a national scale. She did not need to march in the streets. She was, as Dr. King said, already marching in her own way—by showing an entire nation what was true and what was possible.

Advocates for progress come in all forms. Social change is propelled by many people doing many different things that nudge us toward fairer and more inclusive societies. Yet many of us persist in thinking that some approaches are better than others, more real than others, more legitimate than others. We imagine that there is a quintessential version of what an activist should be like and what that activist should do.

A 2020 study of antiausterity activists in Europe, for instance, found that the activists had strict parameters defining who should be part of the movement. "In order to be considered an ideal activist, individuals must do 'enough' of the 'right' type of activism (direct action rather than online activism)," according to researcher Emma Craddock. "The ideal activist identity is underpinned by the distinction participants draw between talking and doing, which feeds into the construction of direct, offline action as the pinnacle of 'real' activism versus online 'slacktivism.'" Activists also judged one another based on their individual lived experiences, judging whether or not someone had the "authority" to speak out or even participate in a given movement.[6]

For anyone, these are incredibly high standards. Most people would fall far short of that ideal. And for those of us who are sensitive, this perceived failure might cause us to feel achingly inadequate or ashamed.

Introverts can feel similarly deficient in cultures that strongly favor extroverted personalities. These cultures aspire to what Susan Cain calls the Extrovert Ideal, or "the omnipresent belief that the ideal self is gregarious, alpha, and comfortable in the spotlight. The archetypal extrovert prefers action to contemplation, risk-taking to heed-taking, certainty to doubt. . . . We like to think that we value individuality, but all too often we admire one type of individual—the kind who's comfortable 'putting himself out there.'"[7]

This isn't too different from what I call the Activist Ideal, which we collectively contribute to and maintain. According to the Activist Ideal, those of us who care about social justice must be bold and fearless. (Even in researching this book, I found many instances of the word *fearless* used to describe individuals dedicated to a cause. This is despite the fact that it is humanly impossible to live without fear. The only known person to ever live without fear had a rare genetic disorder that destroyed large parts of her brain.[8]) The Activist Ideal requires us to be at the front of the march, in the thick of the action, in direct confrontation against the oppressors. The Activist Ideal asks us to always prioritize the needs of those we are serving above our own. The Activist Ideal demands that we persist against every conceivable internal or external obstacle, trying every possible option without ever doubting or giving up. The Activist Ideal requires nothing less than full and total commitment to the cause over the course of our entire lives. And nothing—not our health or our loved ones or risk or danger or the apocalypse itself—should ever weaken that commitment.

Anyone actually living up to this Activist Ideal would be impressive indeed. But it's not possible.

Yet many of us still try to be some version of this idealized model of activism. We swallow our fears and ignore that sick feeling in the pit of our stomach, or we work ourselves to the point of exhaustion, because we think *that is what we are supposed to do*. The thought of falling short of this standard, of potentially disappointing our peers or failing our communities, feels worse to us than the stress and strain we put on ourselves to embody all that the best, most effective activist should be.

The peer pressure in social justice circles to meet the Activist Ideal is immensely strong. In a growing body of research on social activists, scientists have identified a pervasive culture of selflessness and martyrdom in social justice organizations and networks.[9] This entails "a culture of suppressing concerns about activists' well-being altogether," going so far as to "police each other's commitment to causes by belittling attempts at self-care," explain researchers Cher Weixia Chen and Paul C. Gorski of the Center for the Advancement of Well-Being at George Mason University.[10] Chen and Gorski found that activists consistently feel shame and guilt when thinking about their own well-being, and the vast majority reported *never* having a conversation or receiving mentoring about self-care within their organizations. In study after study, activists from many different movements—racial justice, peace, education, LGBTQ rights, and more—consistently report feeling burdened by expectations from within social justice groups.

In an area focused on caring, justice communities have failed to care for one another. We have decided that others deserve our empathy and attention, but we ourselves do not deserve any. We have come to equate dedication with self-sacrifice, and passion with working ourselves into dust. We have created a culture of all or nothing: You are either fully in it—heart, mind, body, and soul, no matter the pain, sacrifices, or consequences—or your contribution doesn't matter. You either change the world, or you fail to do anything at all. We uphold the Activist Ideal as a true reflection of our hearts and souls when it is actually another tool of division, oppression, and control.

Activists themselves admit, and researchers agree, that this culture of all-or-nothing martyrdom is not positive, sustainable, or generative for communities. It does not lead to greater urgency, higher efficiency, or more lasting outcomes. It does not create powerful, unbreakable bonds between team members. Such idealized expectations simply produce an enormous amount of stress for everyone. Yet even those who are aware of the serious consequences of ignoring self-care often get swept up into this way of doing things.[11] Somehow, it feels *right* to suffer alongside those who are suffering. We *should* be investing everything we possibly can into the work of justice, regardless of the consequences.

But this kind of thinking and behavior leads to widespread, chronic burnout in social justice circles. The work itself is already incredibly emotionally intense. Combined with an impossibly high standard of performance and dedication, we create a perfect storm of stress and strain, one that will inevitably take us out one by one.

The cost of burnout is enormous for the individual experiencing it, but it also deeply hurts the very movements and societies we're trying to serve. Many who burn out are forced to significantly reduce their participation or withdraw from justice-oriented work altogether. Their voices, perspectives, skills, gifts, and wisdom become lost to us—and the generations after us. Antiviolence and antipoverty activist Jen Plyler explains the cost: "Instead of figuring out ways to take care of ourselves and each other, social justice groups lose brilliant and committed activists to burnout, disillusionment and poor health. As a result, movements are plagued by fragmentation, lack of reflection and discussion, and 'wheel reinventing' that keeps them from moving their agendas forward."[12]

We all need a different way to serve the social good. We cannot create lasting change if we keep breaking ourselves and one another down. Those who have been doing this work for decades understand this; it's the only way they've been able to continue their efforts. But the tendency to expect superhuman output from mere mortals persists within social justice communities.

Who better to help shift the culture of self-sacrifice within the social justice sphere than sensitive and empathic individuals? We are exactly the right kind of people to support strong, sustainable, restorative activism and self-care. We have the skills and resources to showcase how social change agents come in many forms, from the quieter type of activism we engage in to the more balanced and boundaried way in which we pursue that activism.

To a large extent, we sensitives *must* do things differently. Otherwise we cannot sustainably serve in capacities that speak to our deepest passions and concerns. We risk deeper emotional wounds, greater trauma, and more negative health consequences than our nonsensitive counterparts. And therein lies, in actuality, one of our more remarkable strengths.

We don't seek an alternative approach for ourselves alone; we also do so for the sake of the causes we care so deeply about. We are actually far more effective and can have a more significant impact when we engage in activism in a healthy way—and teach others in our communities to do the same. Educational psychologist Kristin Neff discovered that *self-compassion*, a counterpoint to self-sacrifice, offers profound and positive benefits to ourselves and our communities. Self-compassion strengthens our coping muscles, builds our resilience in the face of challenging and painful experiences, and empowers us to speak out when something isn't right. One study of two hundred women found that those with higher levels of self-compassion felt stronger and more competent, asserted themselves more, and were *more* committed to social activism.[13] As researcher Brené Brown explains, empathy is not finite but multiplicative. "When we practice empathy with ourselves and others, we create more empathy," she says. "The surest way to ensure that you have a reserve of compassion and empathy for others is to attend to your own feelings."[14]

Practicing kindness toward ourselves also allows us to live with a more consistent, holistic ethic. When we listen to our own anxieties and hurts, we become more skilled at listening to the anxieties and hurts of others. When we respond with grace and compassion to ourselves, we become more willing to extend this same grace and compassion to our colleagues, our community, and even our adversaries. We become agents of change not simply by what we do but also by who we are.

Nevertheless, the Activist Ideal persists as the mainstream, accepted standard for sensitives to try to live up to. Being highly attuned to the unspoken expectations placed on us, we are very aware when others approve or disapprove of us. If those around us do not think we are dedicated enough to a cause, we will know it in our bones. Even our unequivocally excellent contributions may be marred by the realization that we have disappointed our colleagues. And since sensitive individuals are idealists, *of course* we want to live up to the ideal promoted by people we respect.

This calls for a great deal of courage to live and be different, even among like-minded peers. We need to learn to advocate for ourselves, setting clear expectations with our supervisors, peers, and colleagues and establishing healthy boundaries between activism, rest, and play. To live in ways that are sustainable, we should listen to our minds and bodies, paying attention when something is out of balance or when we're pushing ourselves too hard.

There is no need to be the ideal activist. No one is the ideal activist. Instead, we can each be activists exactly as we are. Sensitive souls can unhesitatingly embrace the traits within us that nudge us toward healthier, more authentic approaches to changing the world. Our preferences for kindness, empathy, compassion, and a more measured pace will serve us well in taking care of ourselves, supporting our peers, and seeking out the purposes that have been uniquely designed for each of us.

Reflection Questions

1. What kind of social justice activities do you feel like you *should* be doing? Where does the pressure to do these activities come from?
2. Have you witnessed or experienced the expectations of the Activist Ideal in your social justice networks? How does this ideal affect you and others you know?
3. Why do you think it's so tempting to try to live up to an impossible ideal? What steps could you take—for yourself, your colleagues, and your organizations—to begin to counter this ideal?
4. How do you think social justice movements and organizations might change if we collectively embraced a more balanced, sustainable approach? Do you think there might be a cost to doing so?

4

The Resilient Sensitive

"But still, like dust, I'll rise."

Maya Angelou

The night before formally accepting President-elect Franklin Delano Roosevelt's nomination to be secretary of labor, Frances Perkins, feeling the gravity of the role, "cried in deep, wailing sobs that frightened her teenage daughter."[1]

It was 1933. Roosevelt had entrusted Perkins with the herculean task of remaking the American economy in hopes of pulling the country out of the Great Depression. With years of experience as a social worker and advocate in urban workhouses and slums, Perkins well understood the systemic injustices and policy failures that plagued impoverished workers. She also understood the flood of contempt, criticism, hostility, and judgment she would face for being the first-ever female cabinet member and for pushing what was then considered a radical socialist agenda: a forty-hour workweek, a minimum wage, unemployment compensation, a ban on child labor, and health insurance, among other policies meant to benefit workers.[2]

It was a role Perkins felt compelled to accept. And she knew the pressure and emotional toll would be awful. She wept in agony—only hours before she called Roosevelt to accept the nomination. But she had one condition: she would only accept the job if the president supported her entire agenda. Roosevelt was wary of the political fallout, but trusted Perkins and her famously accurate intuition. He agreed to her terms.

Perkins went on to become one of the most consequential secretaries of labor the United States has ever had, serving for an astounding twelve years. She was the true architect of the New Deal, pushing for public works projects that employed millions, raising the overall standard of living for workers, advocating for immigrants and refugees, and creating Social Security. But the job was just as hard as she anticipated, with frequent attacks from politicians, the media, the public, and even fellow cabinet members. She tried to resign multiple times, telling friends she was exhausted from the constant stress, but Roosevelt refused to accept her resignations.[3] Not until Roosevelt passed away and his successor Harry Truman asked for her resignation did she finally depart from the role.[4]

There is always a cost to entering the social justice arena, whether you are at the grassroots level or at the pinnacle of political power. The records of history are, unfortunately, filled with people who lost their freedom or their very lives working toward dignity, well-being, and equality for their fellow human beings.

While most of us likely won't be asked to die for a cause, we will still have to sacrifice. At the very least, we will need to give up time and energy or financial and material resources. Most of us will end up dusty, exhausted, and wounded at some point in our journey.

In recent years, *resilience* has become a central concept across disciplines, showing up in everything from academic journals and TED talks to podcasts and best-selling self-help books. But for those of us who bruise far more easily and need significant time to heal and recover, what does resilience look like in our lives?

The dictionary definition recorded in *Merriam-Webster* says that resilience is "an ability to recover from or adjust easily to misfortune or change."[5] The implication is that the resilient person bounces back quickly, mostly unharmed and unchanged, from any hardship.

I know people like this. They move through life with a Teflon skin, unfazed by challenges, untroubled by the words and actions of others. They are confident and secure, flexible and innovative. They are endlessly optimistic and charge through life with energetic freedom.

I want to be like that—so very much. But I'm not. Not even close. I'm more like Frances Perkins, weeping with fear and anxiety even when I've been handed an amazing opportunity. Hurt and angered by criticism and hostility. Exhausted from stress. Wanting to quit when things get hard. Feeling wounded and worn down long after a stressful season has passed.

For many years, I thought being resilient was simply not a possibility for me. I have burned out far too many times and experienced too much trauma to have that kind of strength and courage. And yet I know if I want to continue serving in the social justice sector in any capacity, I need some measure of resilience. I don't want to fold in on myself at the first sign of hardship. I don't want to have to permanently abandon the work I find so meaningful. And I definitely don't want to experience the cycle of burnout and depression over and over again.

Fortunately, another definition of resilience from author Andrew Zolli in his best-selling book, *Resilience: Why Things Bounce Back*, offers something more. Resilience, according to Zolli, is "the capacity of a system, enterprise, or person to maintain its core purpose and integrity in the face of dramatically changed circumstances."[6] Becoming more resilient, according to social science researchers, depends on a person's *adaptive capacity*, or "the ability to adapt to changed circumstances while fulfilling one's core purpose."[7]

Nowhere in Zolli's—or social science's—definition is the assumption that resilience is quick or easy. It does not require being impervious to hurt, sorrow, or stress. It does not assume the ability to bounce back right away or perpetually feel motivated and hopeful. The truly resilient spirit experiences all kinds of messiness and heartbreak, and maintains persistence and courage. Even in the face of criticism and failure, opposition and doubt, chaos and fear, resilient individuals manage to keep a grasp—however tenuous—on who they are and what they were meant to do. They are defined by a confidence in their calling, not by how well they keep it together.

That means that resilience is possible for all of us. It is not limited by personality or even past trauma. According to the American Psychological Association, "resilience involves behaviors, thoughts, and actions that anyone can learn and develop. The ability to learn resilience is one reason research has shown that resilience is ordinary, not extraordinary."[8] Resilience can be developed and learned not simply through "words or posters," according to Native American studies professor Martin Brokenleg. "What we need are transformative experiences."[9]

If you picked up this book, you probably did so because you know your purpose has something to do with bettering the human condition. But in what area do you want to do that? What communities do you want to serve? Where, when, and how? Determining your calling—or, probably more accurately, series of callings—is a sacred act that requires patience, wisdom, and trial and error. The rest of this book helps explore these questions and offers possibilities so that you can move closer to the freedom song that speaks most to your heart.

There are other questions related to resilience that sensitives and empaths may ask. How do we hold onto our purpose even under great duress? How do we maintain the integrity of our unique personhood when our sensitive nervous systems are mired in intense, stressful, and overwhelming environments?

Shame researcher Brené Brown speaks to a cornerstone of our ability to "rise strong," as she calls it—and that is through *spirituality*. This is not necessarily religion or theology, though it can include a faith tradition. Brown suggests that spirituality is "recognizing and celebrating that we are all inextricably connected to one another by a power greater than all of us, and that our connection to that power and to one another is grounded in love and belonging." When we practice spirituality, she writes, it "brings a sense of perspective, meaning, and purpose to our lives."[10] We see that we are part of something far bigger and greater than ourselves. This perspective and purpose provide an important foundation for us to lean on whenever we meet challenges.

For those of us drawn to social justice, this concept of spirituality is likely already well integrated into how we think and live. We know our well-being is dependent on the well-being of others; we know each person flourishes when we are all flourishing together. In this regard, justice-minded people have a head start on resilience. We already see and connect outside of ourselves, cognizant of the deep and meaningful ways in which we are dependent on one another.

But a broad, abstract understanding of human interconnectedness isn't enough. We need to place ourselves in the narrative as well, in the middle of that web of connection, allowing us to draw from the strength and courage of history and heritage, other people, the universe, or a higher being. Sometimes critical resources of resilience come from our colleagues, communities, and loved ones; other times, it can come from focused silence, solitude, and rest. Tapping into our inner energy and the energy of those around us allows us to grow "resources in the mind," which, according to psychologist Rick Hanson, are essential for building resilience.[11]

Many leaders in fields of social justice, faith, and psychology recommend a rhythm in the activist life that consists of times of activity, balanced with times of rest and restoration. That means to sustain the work of social justice, we need to intentionally take time *not* to engage in social justice. Some faith traditions call this balanced approach *contemplative activism.* We are more grounded when we pursue what Honduran American theologian Jared Alcántara calls "active" practices and "receptive" practices. The active practices of engaging with the world around us ensure we don't become disconnected or apathetic toward others' needs. But, equally important, receptive practices connect us with ourselves and our unique purposes, nourishing our own souls so we can continue to give more to the world.[12] Such receptive practices can include meditation, prayer, breathing exercises, yoga, journaling, walking, and the creative arts.

For those of us more familiar with the go-getter activist model, a slower, more measured approach may seem counterintuitive. But plenty of prominent change agents have taken their restorative time as seriously as their activism. Vinoba Bhave, for example, was a disciple of Gandhi and inherited his spiritual and social mantle. He became a revered social reformer in India in the mid-twentieth century. Across the decades he spoke out for greater equity and inclusion in Indian society. He also spent years at a time in contemplative retreats. Sometimes he went for months without speaking. Yet his influence in advocating for fairer economic and social systems was immense.[13]

The field of psychology provides another framework for understanding why we need this balance. In the early twentieth century, psychologists Robert M. Yerkes and John Dillingham Dodson developed the Yerkes-Dodson law, which explains the relationship between performance and stress.[14] This was later adapted into the simpler Hebbian version.

The Hebbian version says that performance, relative to stress—or *arousal*, as Yerkes and Dodson called it—can be charted on a bell curve. Some measure of stress can push us toward better performance, heightening our senses, sharpening our thinking, and growing our skills. This form of stress is called *eustress*—a term coined by Hungarian endocrinologist Hans Selye—and is characterized by how it energizes, motivates, and excites us.[15] Eustress emerges when we are facing a change or challenge that we want to tackle and feel like we have the capacity to do so. You've likely experienced the almost euphoric feeling of eustress at different points of your life: you feel confident, competent, focused, and empowered.

Eustress is life-giving. It helps foster a sense of purpose and direction, of satisfaction in what we've accomplished and who we are becoming. But it can only happen when we are out in the world, willing to be challenged and open to stepping outside the bounds of what is too easy or comfortable for us.

That said, eustress has a time limit on it. If the stress becomes long term, it begins to feel bigger and more overwhelming. Our minds and bodies become fatigued. The challenges we face that at first energized us begin to surpass our coping abilities and overstretch us, causing a negative form of stress: *distress*.[16] Distress leads to the negative consequences we typically associate with stress, including reduced memory, attention, and problem-solving as well as damage to our mental and physical health.[17]

Generally speaking, sensitive individuals are well equipped to sense when they've passed the bounds of eustress and have entered the territory of distress. Our bodies are already particularly responsive to stimuli, events, and environments; our minds already tend to deeply process what we're experiencing. What's required is that we pay attention to and honor what our neurons and nervous system are trying to communicate. When we're getting signals that we need to take a break, that's essential information to respond to.

That can be difficult when we feel the pressure of pain and suffering and injustice in the world. We may feel responsible for solving each problem we encounter—with every fiber of our being, as long as we draw breath. We want to live up to the Activist Ideal even when we know it's an impossible standard. Activist guilt, that sense that we are never doing enough, is a powerful force.

That's when remembering the importance of a robust spirituality can be a lifeline: you are not alone in this work. You are part of a greater whole. The fate of humanity and the planet does not rest on your shoulders. You are invited to rely on others, just as others rely on you. You deserve, just as you are, time to rest, recover, and receive. You are doing enough. *You* are enough. There is enough empathy to go around for everyone, yourself included.

Yet even when we're trying our best to maintain a healthy rhythm, life can still knock us down. Challenging people, circumstances, or events can cause us deep pain or sorrow. But we can recover. In her book *Rising Strong*, Brené Brown lays out a process for how to get back up after we've been hurt, embarrassed, angered, or otherwise negatively impacted. The things she encourages us to do include (1) naming our feelings and trying to understand the connection between those feelings and our thoughts and behaviors; (2) "revisit[ing], challeng[ing], and reality-check[ing]" the false narratives we've been telling ourselves about our struggles, addressing "topics such as boundaries, shame, blame, resentment, heartbreak, generosity, and forgiveness"; and (3) taking what we've learned and rewriting the ending in a way that is authentic and empowering.[18] This isn't an easy or linear process. The more painful the experience, the longer it will take and the more support we may need along the way. But if we value our own well-being, as well as our ability to do good in the world, it is worthwhile work to do.

It's important to note that these approaches to building our resilience are in response to challenging circumstances, not traumatic ones. When something is so distressing that it impacts our ability to cope and process, we may be experiencing trauma. Trauma, explains psychologist Bessel van der Kolk, is "unbearable and intolerable." We shouldn't try to deal with it on our own. Instead, we need assistance from mentors, spiritual leaders, and mental health professionals.[19] Their expertise and assistance can promote our processing, healing, and recovery.

For a long time, I believed the best defense against painful emotions—grief, shame, embarrassment, disappointment, anger—was to ignore them and push them down. But it is when we face all the messiness of what happened and what we're feeling, when we name how it affected us and what we learned as a result, that their power over us is reduced. "To defend oneself against a fear is simply to [e]nsure that one will, one day, be conquered by it; fears must be faced," civil rights activist James Baldwin wrote.[20] Undergoing this process of facing our fears, facing our painful experiences can actually help rewire our brains. And we grow stronger, steadier, clearer in our sense of purpose and more ready to face the next challenge that comes our way.

Resilience, the ability to hold on to our identity and purpose under challenging circumstances, is possible for all of us. For sensitive individuals, it may take time, practice, and gentleness toward ourselves to nurture this. But it's an invaluable tool in maintaining our health and balance and allowing us to stay in the arena, working toward the social good, for a little longer.

Reflection Questions

1. Do you consider yourself to be a resilient person? Why or why not?
2. If resilience is more about holding onto our identity and purpose than about bouncing back quickly, how might you try to build resilience in yourself?

3. What does it look like when you are being challenged in a healthy way, toward eustress? What are the signs that your eustress is becoming distress?
4. What does healthy spirituality look like for you? What are the beliefs, practices, and communities that keep you most grounded?

5

The Value of Nonsensitive Collaborators

"I would rather walk with a friend in
the dark, than alone in the light."

Helen Keller

In almost every nonprofit or social enterprise job I've had, there was at least one coworker who terrified me. There was the boss who gave me unexpectedly negative feedback on my performance review. There was the director who had sudden, inexplicable outbursts of anger and frustration. There was the colleague who asked pointed, challenging questions, one after the other, staring at me intensely and unrelentingly until I responded to every one of them. There was the manager in another office who frequently sent angry emails in ALL CAPS, punctuated with rows of exclamation marks. There was the direct report who seemed to catch every mistake I made, as if lying in wait for my next screw-up.

Not surprisingly, I had a hard time working with these individuals. They caused me intense stress and anxiety and blunted my confidence and self-esteem. I dreaded my interactions with them. I spent far too many hours rereading email exchanges or mentally replaying conversations, questioning what I could have said or done differently. I would lie awake at night, wondering how or if I could ever fix all the problems they created for me.

Yet, today, with a bit of hindsight, I find that I deeply value those colleagues. I appreciate the challenging experiences they provided, the ways in which they pushed me beyond what was comfortable, and the ways I grew as a result. They were actually agents in helping me build up my resilience.

In any discussion about sensitives and empaths, it is easy to focus on the negative aspects of being around those who aren't like us. Almost every book on empaths references "vampires" of one kind or another—people who suck the life out of you with their harsh words, incessant demands, or insensitive actions. And while it is absolutely vital to set boundaries with toxic people in your life—including in social justice work—it's also healthy to create space for nonsensitive peers who genuinely care about you and the social good. They may come across as prickly or aggressive, but they also bring many gifts to the table.

My nonsensitive colleagues have wowed me time and again with their confidence, persistence, resilience, and risk-taking. They are willing to fight the battles that I can't, taking on the adversaries I would sooner run away from. They aren't afraid to say hard truths or challenge long-held assumptions. They see and pursue opportunities that intimidate me. They help me to see what's possible, and their efforts amplify my own.

Nelson Mandela was such a figure for the anti-apartheid movement in South Africa. While Mandela was quite empathic, he was also revered for his passion and boldness. An amateur boxer earlier in life, Mandela was a leader in opposing apartheid as soon as it was instituted in 1948. He fought the oppressive system through nonviolent means like boycotts, marches, and speeches but also—after the particularly heinous 1960 Sharpeville massacre that killed sixty-nine peaceful protesters—through violent acts of sabotage against strategic targets.

When the Afrikaner Nationalist government called for his arrest in 1961, Mandela went into hiding for seventeen months, donning disguises (including that of a chauffeur), moving constantly, and sometimes stealing out of the country to build support in other African countries. He was finally captured in August 1962 and later sentenced to life in prison.[1] But, even behind bars, he was esteemed as a leader by fellow inmates and prison staff. Mandela was finally released in 1990 and was elected the first Black president of postapartheid South Africa in 1994.[2]

Especially in his years before going to prison, Mandela embodied the warrior-king archetype for the anti-apartheid movement. He was like a general to his (literal and figurative) troops, leading them into battle and inspiring them to take great risks. He acted quickly and confidently, unafraid to make tough, consequential decisions, and was known for being particularly obstinate in his opinions. He was always at the front of the movement, even when he was on the run, continuing to act in audacious ways to oppose and embarrass the government.

He paid a high price for his elevated profile and notoriety—but this also helped him remain effective even after being imprisoned for nearly three decades. Mandela was so influential that most of his followers supported him when, while in prison, he repudiated violence and pushed instead for a peaceful resolution to apartheid. He negotiated with the South African government from behind bars, laying the groundwork for his ascension to the presidency after the transition to a democratic, multiracial democracy.[3]

But Mandela had many partners from all sectors of society in his nearly fifty-year fight against apartheid. Among the most prominent was Anglican Archbishop Desmond Tutu.

At first glance, Mandela and Tutu seemed strikingly similar. Both men were intellectually brilliant. They were personable and gregarious. They demonstrated courage in speaking out against apartheid, and led others to do the same. They both embraced nonviolence and reconciliation in the years after apartheid. And both were awarded the Nobel Peace Prize (Tutu in 1984, Mandela in 1993) for their efforts.

But a closer look reveals that Tutu was, in all likelihood, a highly sensitive soul. According to biographer Shirley du Boulay, Tutu had "a private, introvert side" that required "space and regular periods of quiet."[4] He had a "gentle, caring temperament and would have nothing to do with anything that hurt others."[5] Tutu also relied on his creature comforts, was easily hurt, and was driven by a need to be loved—traits that he expressed embarrassment over and tried to hide from the public.[6] Those characteristics didn't hinder his effectiveness as a leader against apartheid, though his personality likely influenced his very different path to activism.

Tutu, who was born thirteen years after Mandela, began his career as an English and history teacher. When the apartheid system placed significant limits on teachers and schools, he pivoted to become an Anglican priest. Tutu focused on his theological studies as a young man, even as anti-apartheid actions around him grew more intense. He spent time in the United Kingdom, Israel, and Lesotho, furthering his education and taking on teaching duties. It was only in the mid-1970s, after being elected as the first Black dean of St. Mary's Cathedral, Johannesburg (the fourth-highest position in the country's Anglican hierarchy), and after Mandela had already been in prison for more than a decade, that Tutu began speaking out more forcefully and consistently against apartheid.

He spoke from the pulpit; he wrote to the prime minister; he organized prayer vigils and met with movement leaders. As he continued to rise in the ranks within the Anglican Church and broader clergy community, he leveraged his growing influence to speak out, plead for nonviolence on both sides, negotiate with the apartheid government, and garner support from international leaders. After the fall of apartheid, Tutu was appointed by Mandela to lead the Truth and Reconciliation Commission, which acknowledged the great harms committed under apartheid, provided justice for victims, and laid the groundwork for a united South Africa moving forward.[7]

Unlike Mandela, Tutu took time building his career and his platform—thus creating security for himself—before he began to speak more assertively against apartheid. He stayed away from the most aggressive forms of activism and focused on change he could effect within his existing roles. While Tutu's passport was occasionally confiscated by the South African government, and his white congregants were angered by his advocacy, the consequences he faced for his actions were not nearly as severe as Mandela's. His stature as a conscientious and trusted leader within the larger community helped secure his appointment as the chair of the Truth and Reconciliation Commission, where he oversaw a long and complex process of investigating human rights abuses, collecting victim statements, providing an impartial record of past events, and ruling on requests for amnesty.[8]

If we look back, it's clear how the South African anti-apartheid movement benefited from the unique leadership of both men. Together, they were able to challenge the status quo from within the system and outside of it. They were able to speak directly to the oppressed and the oppressors. They appealed to the religious and the secular. When one was not yet ready to engage, the other stoked the fire of activism. When one was imprisoned, the other kept the momentum of the movement going. And, together, they created an inclusive process of healing and justice for a deeply wounded and divided nation.

The anti-apartheid movement would have looked very different, and might not have succeeded, without the important contributions of both men. They needed one another, and South Africa needed them together.

Life may seem easier when we choose to only work with people like us, who think and feel like we do. But that may come with real limitations. You and your sensitive colleagues will probably share similar perspectives and ideas—great for avoiding conflict, but not ideal for problem-solving, innovating, and growing. You may be hurt, frustrated, or overwhelmed by the same people and events. "The disadvantages" in close relationships between HSPs, explains Elaine Aron, "could be that you are more likely to have difficulty doing the same sorts of tasks. . . . So these things tend not to get done."[9] It is far easier to avoid the unpleasant, challenging, or stretching tasks if those around you are also avoiding those same tasks.

The work of social justice is hard. It is discouraging. It is complex and dynamic. We and the causes we care about need people who bounce back more quickly, who eagerly jump into the fray. We need colleagues who are unafraid of making mistakes, are unfazed by failure, and relish confrontation. We need peers who lean toward action and decisiveness. We need people who will challenge our assumptions in private and readily come to our defense in public. Their strengths are a wonderful counterbalance to our strengths; they can help us expand our vision beyond our sensitive lenses.

From my nonsensitive peers, I learned the concept of "good enough" rather than always aiming for perfection. I learned how to try something before having it all planned out. I learned that it's possible for someone to be angry about a situation I'm involved in without their actually being angry at *me*. I learned that a very legitimate response to making a mistake is to briefly reflect on my learnings and then move on. I learned that failures—even big, ugly, hairy ones—don't have to mean the end of anything. I learned that hope and grief, affection and frustration, and imperfection and success can all coexist.

I haven't stopped being sensitive after working alongside nonsensitive colleagues. I still have trouble with criticism and strongly worded emails. But I'd like to think that I'm a healthier version of my highly sensitive self: willing to take action a little sooner and better at understanding what's worth processing and what's worth letting go.

We priestly advisers need warrior activists in our lives to buoy, encourage, inspire, and sometimes defend us. This is particularly true in a sphere like social justice, where some measure of conflict and resistance is inevitable. As they take on the louder, messier fights, they create space for us to work in quieter, more subtle ways. They charge at a problem from the front while we can sneak at it from the side. Their blind spots are our strengths and vice versa. The sustainability of movements and the potential for social change is far greater when those of differing temperaments choose to work together. When we can truly respect and appreciate our differences, and create space for one another's skills and gifts, there's so much more we can accomplish.

Of course, it is still challenging to partner with nonsensitive colleagues. They are far more likely to overstimulate us or stress us out with their strong opinions, quick actions, and limited empathy. Just as we cannot fully understand how they think, feel, and behave, they cannot understand how their words and actions might affect us.

Work expert Barrie Jaeger encourages us to become well versed in our own signs of stress and overstimulation, so we know when we need to take a step back and find a quiet space to center ourselves and regather our thoughts.[10] "Recovery time for people-related stress is very long compared to milder forms of stress," she explains.[11] We absolutely can and should take breaks from our well-meaning but overwhelming peers when we need to. And we should feel empowered to be our own best advocate: saying no, setting boundaries, explaining our preferred communication styles, and letting colleagues know when they are out of line. The more we engage in these healthy practices, the easier they will become—and the more likely we can enjoy working alongside those who don't share our sensitivities.

Like Tutu, we may at times feel embarrassed or ashamed about the traits that come with being highly sensitive or empathic. We may feel like we are much further from the Activist Ideal than most of our peers. (Remember that at least 80 percent of the population is not highly sensitive.) Henri Nouwen, Dutch priest, professor, and advocate for people with disabilities, observes that "competition, not compassion, is our main motivation in life." We instinctively want to know how we measure up—and, unfortunately, that distracts us from what actually matters. "This all-pervasive competition," Nouwen says, "which reaches into the smallest corners of our relationships, prevents us from entering into full solidarity with each other, and stands in the way of our being compassionate."[12] We cannot truly work together toward a shared goal if we are intent on focusing on our differences and shortcomings. Our causes suffer when we fixate on what we don't like about each other rather than the oppressive laws, systems, and behaviors that perpetuate injustice.

And our causes suffer when we try to be too much like one another instead of leveraging the vast range of skills and perspectives that we each bring to the table. "A minority is powerless while it conforms to the majority," wrote abolitionist Henry David Thoreau in his classic essay *Civil Disobedience*.[13] For sensitives and empaths, our power is in our difference. Our power is in the particular qualities and gifts we carry as heart- and gut-centered individuals, in our ability to do, see, and feel things that most others can't. There is no social justice effort that would be served only by activists of identical temperaments.

Working with those who aren't as sensitive, even the most well intentioned among them, will inevitably result in tension, conflict, and stress. I have experienced plenty of this tension, and you probably have too. This does not always have to be negative. Like the sharpening of iron, this friction—when it comes from a place of mutual respect and shared passion for a cause—can better our ideas, strategies, and collaboration.

I'm sure Nelson Mandela and Desmond Tutu had fierce disagreements over strategy, tactics, and approaches as well as irritations over personality differences. They probably needed time away from each other to get perspective and recover. But each continued to welcome the other as an invaluable partner in common goals, inviting collaboration time and again. No doubt their impact was enhanced by their differences.

One of Tutu's many contributions to the world was the popularization of the African philosophy called *ubuntu*. Roughly translated as "I am because you are" or "I am human only because you are human," ubuntu refers to our shared humanity and our interdependence.[14] The priestly advisers are because the warrior leaders are. We are invaluable; so are they. And we are all more effective advocates for change when we balance one another, challenge one another, and encourage one another toward the next step in the journey.

Reflection Questions

1. What peers, colleagues, and fellow volunteers have you found most challenging to work with? What have you appreciated about working with them?
2. What have you learned from partnering with people who are less sensitive or less empathic? What else would you like to learn from them?
3. What kinds of expectations and boundaries do you need to set with your nonsensitive colleagues to ensure healthy communication and collaboration?
4. What could healthy, refining conflict look like when you are working with others with very different personalities?

Part II

Considerations and Questions

6

Pursuing Activism as You Are

"I alone cannot change the world, but I can cast a stone across the waters to create many ripples."

Mother Teresa

A few years ago, I got into a Twitter fight with a stranger about the United States' immigration policy that severely limited the number of refugees accepted into the country. We only exchanged about ten messages, and by social media standards, our back-and-forth was relatively cordial. But I agonized over each of my tweets; I experienced heart palpitations each time the other woman responded. I couldn't stop thinking about the discussion, critiquing each of my words and wincing at each of hers. It was, in a word, awful—and I've never done it again.

In recent years, there's been a big push to engage with justice issues online, especially on social media. Everything about our online persona can be leveraged for a cause: hashtags, posts, tweets, retweets, memes, quotes, profile images, frames of profile images, whom we follow, who follows us, black squares, white squares, red squares, rainbow flags, upside-down flags, and much, much more.

Social media has certainly played a significant role in raising awareness about important movements, including #MeToo, Black Lives Matter, and the Arab Spring. It has been the primary conduit for ensuring that horrific acts of injustice, such as the killing of George Floyd, go viral and attract global attention. But as a whole, social media activism has a poor track record of catalyzing long-term change. By itself, it is not going to transform societies.[1] And when considered in balance with the grave damage that social media has caused through spreading disinformation and conspiracy theories, coalescing hate groups, increasing anxiety and depression, doxxing and compromising privacy, giving predators access to victims, and online bullying, it's fair to ask whether social media is actually serving us well.

I have seen people castigated online for what they promoted or defended. I have seen people torn apart for not saying anything. I have witnessed people being criticized for saying something but in the wrong way or at the wrong time; others have suffered huge blowback for a misunderstanding or even a typo.

The online world is often not a friendly place. It can be impersonal and cruel. It offers limited opportunity for sincere discourse and infinite possibilities for harm and emotional scarring. For those deeply motivated to engage in digital debates, or those who enjoy them, I will gladly cheer you on. Humanity certainly needs more voices of reason, justice, and compassion in the online world.

But if you don't want to raise your voice online, then don't. Regardless of what the activists you know may say, you don't *have* to fight for social justice online. You don't have to publicly air your political disagreements with your friends or family members. You don't have to shoot zingers at opposing groups. You don't have to use the latest popular hashtag or change your profile picture each time there's a major news event.

One of the greatest opportunities and challenges for sensitive justice advocates is to find meaningful forms of engagement that uniquely fit us. It will probably not look like what most activists are doing because most activists are not sensitive and empathic to the same degree. It could very well involve building your own role or charting your own path, one that may or may not be understandable to those around you.

This could be a terrifying prospect—but also, hopefully, an exhilarating one with wide-open possibilities. I firmly believe there is a reason why we each are the way we are. We each bring unique gifts, talents, and insights into the world that no one else can contribute.

History is full of social justice heroes who have carved their own particular niches, operated on their own timelines, and spoken up for change through different avenues and at different volumes. They have done so in almost every imaginable role and sector, across geography and social status and other demographics. They have been advocates and activists in their neighborhoods, workplaces, schools, government agencies, houses of worship, networks, and within their own families. They have pursued what we might consider to be small or quiet activities, but often for the sake of a big and meaningful cause.

We too can find creative ways to contribute toward social progress exactly where we are and with those already around us. Employers or hiring managers who fill roles in organizations make decisions that absolutely matter and affect entire teams. Those who spend significant time in a space that is not sufficiently diverse support change by reaching out to support or mentor members of underrepresented groups. Those working in an organization where worker rights and benefits are not equitable or fair have the opportunity to advocate for better working conditions there and in the wider industry. If you are a parent, grandparent, godparent, foster parent, guardian, coach, or mentor, what you teach little ones in your life about what is right and fair, what is good and courageous is part of their formation and changes the course of their lives. If you have influence over others, either in digital spaces or in person, you have the opportunity to offer hope and guidance and inspiration. The options and opportunities for creating change in your part of the world are endless.

The reality is that the Activist Ideal will never stop demanding more of us. What we give will never be enough. Even when we have sacrificed every earthly possession and every cell in our body, it will still not be enough. Perhaps we are driven by the misguided notion that large-scale revolutionary progress can and should happen *now*. That societies can be entirely transformed *if I just work harder*. We expect social progress to take place exactly when, where, and in the manner we want it to.

Very occasionally, a corrupt ruler or a damaging policy might be toppled in a short amount of time. But systemic change almost always takes far longer. All of the social movements we are most familiar with took decades of sustained activism before substantial progress was achieved—and that progress often came through a meandering, unexpected route. No one could have predicted exactly what series of actions or events would eventually turn the tide. And many of those movements, such as abolitionism, civil rights, women's rights, disability rights, and LGBTQ rights, are ongoing and likely will be for years to come.

That is why the question of *sustainability* is so important—both for individual activists and for entire movements. While it would be wonderful for social progress to come quickly, we do not need to despair if that doesn't happen. It is not incumbent on any one of us to drastically change the world in a single generation. We can, though, consider how we create meaningful incremental change and how we lay the foundation for future change. What we do now can reverberate far beyond our individual actions and our present moment.

The Seventh Generation principle, based on the ancient philosophy of the indigenous Haudenosaunee Confederacy, encourages us to make decisions now that will be sustainable even seven generations into the future.[2] While the principle has been applied most commonly to environmental concerns—how to use our precious natural resources wisely and sustainably—its relevance extends into many other areas of life. As we look toward long-term social change, we can remind ourselves that many passionate, caring people will come after us. We can recognize that our choices and actions today might make a big difference in *their* chances of success.

Khalida Brohi, a Pakistani women's activist, had the opportunity to grow into her calling primarily because her father chose to buck traditional customs. He refused to marry her off as a child bride, even when his father—her grandfather—requested it. He chose to educate his daughters just as he educated his sons, a highly unusual choice in their traditional community. As a result, when Brohi's cousin was murdered in a horrific honor killing, Brohi knew how to use the power of social media and protests to demand justice for her cousin and women like her, as well as to demand better legal protections for all Pakistani women.[3]

Without her father's choices, her impact would not have been possible. Sikander Jattak advocated for his own children first. Jattak came from a very humble background, with limited opportunities for education and employment, but that didn't stop him from building a revolution in his own home. The world needs parents like this—just as we need neighbors, friends, coworkers, community members, volunteers, and mentors—dedicated to nudging our societies toward greater equity and inclusion. Their contributions may or may not be recorded in history books, but we are all beneficiaries of their heartfelt labor.

The path toward social justice is lined with the meaningful choices, actions, and words of individuals, families, and communities who did something brave and generous with the resources they were given. Never underestimate, for example, the importance of simply entering and existing in spaces not previously known for being inclusive. We consider Jackie Robinson, Sally Ride, Helen Keller, and Sidney Poitier to be pioneers and ceiling-smashers for breaking the status quo in their respective fields. There are many others who aren't as prominent but are just as important: Edith Clarke (the first woman to earn a degree in electrical engineering), Bill Tilden (the first openly gay professional athlete), Clifton Wharton (the first Black CEO of a major US corporation), Severo Ochoa (the first Latino to win a Nobel Prize in physiology or medicine), Ignatius Wang (the first Asian American bishop of the Roman Catholic Church), and Judith Heumann (the first New York City public school teacher in a wheelchair), to name only a few. Their decision to persevere in roles, fields, sectors, and industries where they were not initially welcomed formed cracks in long-standing walls of prejudice, intolerance, discrimination, and hate.

These individuals, who asked for little more than to be accepted as they were in their vocations of choice, played a critical role in laying down trails of change, surfacing the path, and making it easier for others to follow.

Sometimes, your role in social change comes to you. Richard Loving and Mildred Jeter, for example, only wanted to be legally married and allowed to live together in their home state. Richard, who was white, and Mildred, who was African American and Native American, were longtime friends who fell in love in the ethnically diverse town of Central Point, Virginia. Mixed-race marriage, or miscegenation, was not allowed in Virginia in 1958, so the two married in nearby Washington, DC, where it was legal. But they were arrested for committing a felony shortly after returning to Virginia. In lieu of a jail sentence, they were forced to leave the state.

By all accounts, Richard and Mildred were quiet, unassuming people. They were not the type to seek attention or look for a fight. But they desperately wanted to return home to

Virginia. In 1963, Mildred wrote a letter to then-US attorney general Robert F. Kennedy, asking for help. He connected her to the American Civil Liberties Union, which took their case. In what became known as *Loving v. Virginia*, the Supreme Court in 1967 unanimously struck down laws banning interracial marriage across the country.[4] The decision ensured a key civil right for countless families then and now.

The Lovings did not plan to become activists or civil rights icons. But they wanted to be able to exercise their basic rights; they were willing to ask for help in fighting for those rights; and they remained dedicated to the cause until what they deserved was granted to them.

Finding your own way in social justice work requires courage, creativity, wisdom, and an openness to possibility. It requires shaking off the unhealthy and unrealistic expectations of others. It asks us to embrace our differences as beautiful and our unique personalities and perspectives as gifts, rather than comparing ourselves to others. It requires discernment: knowing when to step into the arena and when to step back, when to forge a new path and when to walk a well-worn trail. When we respond to what our bodies, hearts, life circumstances, and environments tell us about how we can sustainably and meaningfully serve the public good—in that moment, we have all we need and bring exactly who we are.

But how can we know these things? There's a reason why every book, guide, course, training, or coaching program about purpose and vocation begins at the same place: *know thyself*. We can be surprisingly ignorant about our own needs, desires, hurts, and dreams unless we take the time to sit with ourselves. Unless we allow ourselves to wonder, question, reflect, and dig deep.

In his classic book, *Let Your Life Speak: Listening for the Voice of Vocation*, education reformer Parker J. Palmer explains how the Quaker phrase that inspired the title of his book holds meaning for him: "Before you tell your life what you intend to do with it, listen for what it intends to do with you. Before you tell your life what truths and values you have decided to live up to, let your life tell you what truths you embody, what values you represent."[5]

Finding your place in the social justice sphere is not about conforming to someone else's version of who you need to be. It's not about contorting yourself to fit a particular role or activity that seems especially noble or effective. Finding your call begins with finding yourself. "There is something in every one of you that waits and listens for the sound of the genuine in yourself," said philosopher, theologian, and civil rights advocate Howard Thurman. "It is the only true guide you will ever have. And if you cannot hear it, you will all of your life spend your days on the ends of strings that somebody else pulls."[6]

There have been times in my life when I thought the work of growing my self-awareness and self-understanding was selfish. I thought navel-gazing was a waste of time when the world was burning and people were suffering. But I've come to understand that the inner work of the heart is as much a part of social justice as the advocacy in the streets. Only when you can see who you authentically are can you begin to grasp what meaning and purpose look like for you. And only then can you live out the best version of yourself, which is what humanity most needs from you.

Before we begin to pursue these answers, it's a good idea to consider which questions to ask first. In the next four chapters, we'll look at different lenses through which to see our distinct role in the social justice sphere. The age-old questions of *what, who, when*, and *where* provide a helpful framework for thinking through the conditions that could help us operate best in social justice. They will help us consider the needs, interests, and limitations that drive each of us. We'll look at the possibilities and pitfalls that sensitives can encounter as they attempt to contribute to social progress. And each chapter ends with a series of questions you may want to consider. You might want to ponder these questions in concert with other helpful tools like personality assessments, career guides, life coaching, therapy, spiritual direction, and more.

If you are interested in understanding more about your particular sensitivity and empathy, you can also review the appendix, which explores different subsets of the highly sensitive and empathic, and can help you think through traits that are unique to you.

My hope is that, when brought together, these various lenses will create a kaleidoscope of options for exploration—both within you and outside you. Perhaps you will leave with more questions than answers. That's perfectly fine. You don't need to have your entire social justice path figured out. You just need to look toward your very next step.

7

What

Discovering Purpose without Being Confined by It

"What am I living for and what am I dying for are the same question."

Margaret Atwood

Juliette Hampton Morgan could have been like any of the aristocratic Southern belles of her time. Born in 1914, she was the only child of an affluent, influential family in Montgomery, Alabama. But there was something about Morgan that set her apart from many of her peers: she suffered from severe anxiety. Her anxiety attacks were so debilitating that she couldn't drive, so she rode the city bus to work—first as a teacher and later as a librarian.

During her daily commute, Morgan witnessed the frequent injustices, cruelties, and humiliations that African Americans experienced on the segregated buses of Montgomery. One day a Black female passenger paid her ten-cent fare at the front of the bus, and as the law required, she stepped off the bus to reenter through the back door. As she headed to the back door, the bus driver began speeding away, leaving the woman behind.

A furious Morgan pulled the emergency cord and demanded that the bus driver stop to allow the woman to board. Such defiance to the Jim Crow system by a white woman was unheard of in deeply segregated Alabama. But Morgan persisted that day and for days afterward, pulling the emergency cord each time she witnessed a similar injustice. She also wrote letters to her local newspaper, the *Montgomery Advertiser*, calling for a change in busing laws, for federal antilynching laws, and the abolishment of the poll tax. After Rosa Parks's 1955 arrest for refusing to give up her seat on a bus, Morgan wrote a letter to the newspaper in support of Parks's act of resistance—the only white voice in all of Montgomery willing to publicly oppose segregation.[1]

Morgan, it seems, did not plan to become a civil rights activist. She did not develop a clear strategy or establish a civil rights organization. She did not go about building a team or soliciting donations. She simply responded instinctively to the injustices she saw in her own community, taking hold of whatever opportunities she had to speak out.

This in-the-moment approach was a far cry from the careful way I approached social justice work in my twenties. I told myself that if I was going to change the world, I couldn't just approach it off the cuff. I had to plan and strategize and know exactly what I was doing. Back then, I was obsessed with questions of *what.* What issue was I most passionate about? What kind of work would have the most impact? What role would best fit my skills while also benefiting my career? What title and salary did I need? What did I want my legacy to be?

If there wasn't a strategic plan in place for myself or a proven model of change for the cause, I did not want to do it. If something was not going to have a significant impact on a massive scale, I didn't even want to consider it. I worried constantly that ending up in the "wrong" social justice job, organization, or field could derail my life purpose. It was a fundamentally flawed and anxiety-inducing framework for evaluating what social justice activities I should do.

I now understand that there is not just one right answer to the question of what someone should do within the social justice realm. There are actually many possible answers, each as legitimate and worthy as the next. Among the 204 sensitive and empathic individuals I surveyed, 161 had previously engaged in social justice activities. These respondents listed nearly fifty different issues they had been involved with. The majority of them had engaged with three or more distinct causes.

In our complex, interwoven societies, almost every issue area intersects with a dozen others. Every strategy or solution can be pursued through different plans or programs. The change agent who cares deeply about children, for example, may consider pursuing change in education and health as well as racial justice, affordable housing, immigration, and climate change. The activist who wants to support criminal justice reform may look at the legal or political sectors but also community-police relations, early intervention strategies, academic research, public education, advocacy, and support programs for the formerly incarcerated.

We may each have a general sense of what we are wired to do, but it doesn't have to be defined so narrowly. We can choose and experiment—and feel free to leave behind what does not nurture our minds, bodies, and souls. As I've researched the lives of activists and social justice heroes, I've discovered many were catalyzed into action by serendipitous events, happy accidents, chance encounters, and unexpected losses—and just as many of them experienced digressions, detours, and pit stops along the way.

If you find yourself hopping from one justice issue to another, or trying on various roles or activities, or taking hold of new opportunities as they come, you are in excellent company. Juliette Hampton Morgan's civil rights résumé was not a linear progression of activism but a patchwork of ad hoc activities scattered across nearly two decades. Yet those activities coalesced into a larger impact, such that she was recognized by Martin Luther King Jr. as a significant influence on his work and the movement he spearheaded.[2]

We can, of course, still have a strategic approach to answering the question of *what* to do. It's wise to consider what issue areas you care most about and what roles might best fit your personality, skills, interests, experience, and desire for growth. It's a good idea to peruse job boards and volunteer listings, talk to wise friends and mentors, conduct informational interviews, and do your research. Each of these activities will help you better understand yourself, your interests, and how they might intersect with the needs around you.

But it is also wise to free ourselves from the notion that there is a perfect job, role, activity, or movement out there for each of us. This ideal does not exist; no role is ever perfect or permanent. If we let idealism—about the perfect job or action or movement—drive our decision-making, that may lead us to focus exclusively on what we think we *should* do or how we can change society without truly evaluating if it makes sense for us. It also may put blinders on us, preventing us from seeing those serendipitous moments or detours that can open new ideas and directions for us.

Relying exclusively on our idealism, according to work expert Dr. Barrie Jaeger, is one of the "big mistakes" that highly sensitive people make when it comes to choosing work. We have a deep need to make a positive difference, and that need gets prioritized over other important needs. According to Jaeger, HSPs are prone to "taking on a job out of a need for meaning and our own idealism. These are powerful incentives that can sugarcoat a bitter circumstance enough for us to endure it well past the point where we have begun to pay a price."[3]

We pay that price when our work becomes what Jaeger calls *drudgery*. Drudgery is not simply about being bored, though it can include that. Roles that lead us into drudgery deplete far more energy than they give to us; they often involve difficult, intractable people or problems; they make us feel restricted, unappreciated, or disrespected.[4]

Drudgery sounds mild, but it can have immensely serious consequences, including burnout and depression. The most objectively meaningful role in the world can still sap us of our joy and energy if it does not match who we are and what we can give.

The story of journalist and activist Iris Chang is a sobering reminder of this. She is best known for writing the 1997 international best seller *The Rape of Nanking: The Forgotten Holocaust of World War II.* Motivated by her own grandparents' escape from the city of Nanking in China (now called Nanjing), Chang spent three years interviewing survivors and meticulously researching human rights abuses by reading through diaries, letters, and original source materials.[5] Chang's book chronicled how, in under two months in 1937, more than 300,000 Chinese civilians were murdered and 80,000 women and girls were systematically raped by the Imperial Japanese Army.[6] In the intervening six decades, few in the international community, including the Chinese and Japanese governments, acknowledged what had happened. The genocide and trauma of hundreds of thousands of Chinese were silenced and ignored until Chang's book—filled with searing firsthand accounts, unsparingly graphic details, and Chang's pronounced outrage—exploded onto the scene.

When it was released, a *New York Times* review called *The Rape of Nanking* an "important new book" that raised "several troubling questions." Among them: "How could such mass barbarity have remained so neglected by historians for so long? Why have the Chinese never asked Japan for reparations? How could the Japanese Army have engaged in such a monstrous and protracted crime against humanity with so little evident awareness of the moral significance of what it was doing?"[7]

But for Chang, the personal cost was immense. Seven years after the release of *The Rape of Nanking*, after she had published a second successful book and was researching the Bataan Death March for yet another, Iris Chang took her own life. She was only thirty-six years old. Her friends and family later reported that she had been anxious and deeply depressed for months prior to her death.[8]

Chang had received much acclaim for her work, becoming a sought-after speaker and a vocal activist for reparations from the Japanese government. But the growing pain, grief, and despair from her work outweighed all that. The significant good she did could not erase the secondary trauma she experienced as she documented the worst of human evil.

Secondary trauma, according to psychologists Rose Zimering and Suzy Bird Gulliver, is "indirect exposure to trauma through a firsthand account or narrative of a traumatic event."[9] It has also been called *compassion fatigue*, *empathy fatigue*, or *vicarious traumatization*. Anyone who engages with traumatized individuals—therapists, health care workers, social workers, journalists, investigators, educators, and more—is at risk for secondary trauma. And without sufficient training or adequate professional and personal support, or when there is close identification with the survivors, the risk of secondary trauma only increases.[10]

"Empathy fatigue," explains psychologist Susan Albers, "is a person's inability to care" due to "repeated exposure to stressful or traumatic events." Emotional symptoms can include isolation, apathy, feeling overwhelmed or hopeless, depression, and guilt. Physical symptoms can include headaches, nausea, trouble sleeping, changes in appetite, and exhaustion.[11] For deeply empathic people, secondary trauma can hit us faster, harder, and deeper, and take far longer to recover from.

While all justice issues are valid to consider, it's important to remember that some issues may be more heartrending for us than others. Genocide, human trafficking, war crimes, racial violence, sexual violence, and child abuse, for example, are urgent issues that deserve significant attention and the best minds and hearts we can spare toward prevention and justice. But they are also areas of great brutality, cruelty, and evil. They have the potential to claim even more victims through secondary trauma, if we are not equipped to manage the pain and suffering we encounter.

So, as you consider what it is you want to do in the social justice sector, consider beginning with what you *don't* want to do. What will cause you secondary trauma or empathy fatigue? What social issues are too heartbreaking, painful, or triggering for you? What or who might you identify so closely with that they become wounding for you?

In addition, it's important to ask yourself what kinds of jobs or responsibilities will cause you far too much stress. Every justice activity will require time and energy. Will they be healthy expenditures of personal resources, or will they also lead to burnout or exhaustion? Highly sensitive blogger and podcaster Kelly O'Laughlin suggests that sensitives avoid particular types of roles, especially ones that:

- focus on getting quantitative results, like hitting numbers and sales targets;
- involve regular forms of confrontation, negotiation, or debate;
- take place in loud, chaotic environments or involve loud, chaotic events; or
- require extensive, intensive interactions with people without sufficient alone time for recovery.[12]

This doesn't mean you can't consider a job or volunteer role that involves these elements. Some sensitives can tolerate certain stresses better than others; some may have a higher tolerance for stress at one life stage more than at others. We can give ourselves the grace to learn over time what works for us and what doesn't; that will invariably involve trial and error. The more we pay attention to ourselves and our physical and emotional responses to different contexts, the better equipped we will be to avoid the kinds of social justice work that require too much.

Of course, knowing what to avoid provides only part of the answer of what to do. The other key component is exploring what makes your spirit sing. The most sustainable justice work overlaps significantly with what you love to do. Working for the social good is not about self-sacrifice and giving up everything that brings you joy. It is not about adding your own suffering to the suffering you are trying to alleviate. "Don't ask what the world needs," advised Howard Thurman. "Ask what makes you come alive, and go do it. Because what the world needs is people who have come alive."[13]

What makes you come alive may seem like it has nothing to do with the most urgent justice issues of our day—but it's still worth leaning into because it can reveal your specific calling and gifts. Throughout history, creative and unconventional approaches have catalyzed generations of social change. Consider your hobbies, special talents, interests, recreational activities, favorite social circles, most-loved places and environments, what you always wish you had more time for—and use that as a starting point for building a role that you can wear comfortably and authentically.

This will all take time. It will take time to understand yourself, your limitations, and your joys. It will take time to find the type of social justice activity or career that fits your unique traits and talents. That is to be expected. If it helps, take advantage of the many personality assessments and frameworks available out there (I've included some in the appendix), as well as professional resources like life coaches and therapists, to fill in the details of who you are.

In the meantime, it's okay to try, explore, move toward, or walk away from different roles and activities in the social justice realm. Your answers to the *what* questions will probably be nothing like mine, and that is a wonderful thing. There is not one way or one answer, not a singular strategy or program, to how you can change the world. Your uniqueness, defined by your strengths, limitations, and the particular way you approach justice work, is your greatest asset for a planet in need.

***What* questions to consider:**

- What social issues do I find myself drawn to?
- What social issues do I have a personal stake or interest in?
- What social issues do I really want to understand and learn more about?
- What injustice is too hard for me to even hear about, let alone spend time working on?
- Do I prefer to be very focused on a specific, narrowly defined cause, or do I prefer to address large-scale issues?
- What issues have I worked on in the past? Did I enjoy focusing on them or not?
- What specific skills or experiences am I interested in developing?
- What activities or hobbies do I always wish I had more time for? Is there a way to incorporate that into my social justice engagement?
- What types of responsibilities or activities cause me the most stress?
- What types of responsibilities or activities do I enjoy the most?
- What social justice role or activity am I curious about? Is there someone I can ask about this?
- What is my tolerance for risk in taking on a job that may or may not be a good fit?
- What volunteer roles can I try on for size?

8

Who

Sources of Great Strength or Great Harm

"Never doubt that a small group of thoughtful,
committed people can change the world.
Indeed it is the only thing that ever has."
Margaret Mead

The peace movement, one would think, would be an excellent place to find congenial, collaborative colleagues. Not necessarily. In a 1992 qualitative study by psychologist Mary E. Gomes, published in the *Journal of Humanistic Psychology*, seventy-five peace activists in the San Francisco Bay Area reported that their greatest rewards and greatest stresses came from the same source: their fellow activists.

Connecting with fellow activists, according to 68 percent of respondents, was the best part of engaging in the peace movement. They enjoyed "meeting inspiring people" and experiencing a "sense of community" and "sense of solidarity."

But almost as many, 57 percent, reported that other activists caused them significant stress. Among the specific stressors caused by fellow activists were factionalism, personality conflicts, unrealistic commitment expectations, self-righteous attitudes, and, ironically, "intolerance." Study participants demonstrated this very intolerance with harsh critiques of their peers for their egos, incompetence, limited experience, and lack of commitment.[1] In other words, there wasn't much peace *between* the activists, even as they strived for peace on a global scale.

Conflict between people is inevitable. Every human sees and experiences life differently; as a result, we are bound to disagree with one another occasionally. And the more we care about something, the more likely we are to dig into our positions and hold fast to our perspectives, certain that *our* thoughts, ideas, and perspectives are better than someone else's.

Across social movements, infighting has pretty much been the norm. Disagreements about anything from strategies and goals to responsibilities and leadership often turn into fiery, divisive arguments. American women's suffrage activists and advocates for the African American vote, once powerful allies, ended up parting ways after the Fifteenth Amendment, which gave only men the right to vote.[2] After the Nineteenth Amendment gave all American women the right to vote, many white women, despite their previous collaborations with Black women, parted ways with women of color, who were still largely excluded from casting ballots.[3] The LGBTQ rights movement in the 1970s divided gay, lesbian, and trans individuals, with each group aiming for different goals and mistrusting the other.[4] Within the disability community today, ongoing disagreements are driven by complex questions around how to perceive disabilities (embrace or overcome?) and how to advocate for their community (as subgroups, as one collective, or in collaboration with other marginalized communities?).[5] Across the centuries, the debate between violent and nonviolent approaches in activism has raged, from abolitionism and civil rights to Native rights and environmental justice.

But within our approach to disagreements is a vast range of difference—from healthy debate to toxic conflict, from tolerating different perspectives to throwing collaborators under the bus. That's why, whatever your cause, the people you choose to surround yourself with are of the utmost importance. Their character, conversation, and collaboration will deeply affect you. Who they are and how they interact with you can determine whether a job or activity is a positive experience or an awful one.

This is true for individuals in any area of work. "In general, people leave their jobs because they don't like their boss, don't see opportunities for promotion or growth, or are offered a better gig (and often higher pay)," according to the *Harvard Business Review*.[6] Individuals burn out on the job when they are routinely disrespected or pressured to stay connected to their work after hours.[7] Even volunteers are far more likely to quit when their voices aren't heard, their responsibilities aren't clear, they aren't appreciated, or they don't feel like part of the team.[8] Among the respondents to my survey who had burned out, about 30 percent cited a bad boss or leader within the organization as a key cause. Fifteen percent reported being personally or professionally attacked by colleagues *from their own organization.*

And what keeps people in roles? In my survey, nearly five in ten respondents who had had a positive social justice experience cited supportive, meaningful relationships and a strong team as major contributors. This was one of the most common reasons given for a positive experience, second only to seeing the impact of their efforts. Whether you are a volunteer, contractor, part-time or full-time employee, your experience will be deeply influenced by the colleagues around you and the organizational culture they help create. Beyond the *what* of our efforts, *whom* we're doing it with and *whom* we're doing it for affect how the organization or group is run, and, therefore, how it makes us feel.

This is especially true for sensitive individuals, who have a knack for noticing what isn't working well or isn't right or fair and are deeply affected by toxic cultures, hostile relationships, and low morale. Being part of an unhealthy organization, even when it's having a big impact in the world, is not sustainable. Nor is it healthy to stay in a meaningful role while working for a disrespectful supervisor or a dysfunctional team. Such contexts can cause emotional scarring and burnout over the long run. And because sensitive people tend to have trouble leaving or quitting something we've committed to, it's far better to be aware of these risks before jumping in.[9]

Unfortunately, the nonprofit sector is full of organizations that aren't optimally run. The Stanford Survey on Leadership and Management in the Nonprofit Sector found that four out of five nonprofits in the United States have leadership and management issues.[10] Anywhere from 25 to 33 percent of nonprofits struggle with rewarding high performance, providing helpful feedback, and setting clear expectations for team members. NGOs in other countries have also been found to falter in staff management, staff development, communication and coordination, and operational expertise.[11]

There are no flawless groups or organizations; there are no perfect leaders or managers. Even the most successful, prolific, and admirable social justice hero may not always treat others well. Labor organizer Cesar Chavez, for example, was notoriously controlling and refused to delegate authority or responsibility to those around him. United Farm Workers (UFW) employees had grueling hours and received little to no wages, making their work unsustainable or even impossible when they had families to support.[12] Chavez tended to make staffing decisions based on "whim and fancy and not on facts."[13] As a result, the turnover among his lieutenants and aides was significant, especially in his later years.

Chavez is not the only social justice icon who made poor decisions or acted hypocritically. Nelson Mandela, recognized for advancing women's rights in South Africa, was accused of chauvinism, choosing to surround himself with beautiful women at work whom he would regularly flirt with.[14] Martin Luther King Jr. allowed Bayard Rustin, one of the civil rights movement's most talented organizers, to mostly serve behind the scenes, sometimes without due credit, because Rustin was openly gay. King and other leaders feared Rustin's sexual orientation would damage the movement and, at times, considered forcing him out.[15] Gandhi first came to prominence as a lawyer in South Africa, arguing that those from India should be treated more like whites and not like "Natives of Africa."[16] While he later became decidedly anti-racist, Gandhi held other controversial views: He argued that Jainism and Sikhism were not their own religions but part of Hinduism. After World War II, Gandhi said that Jews should have committed collective suicide as an act of heroism to arouse the sympathies of the world toward the Holocaust.[17]

These examples are not meant to diminish the legacy of these leaders but to remind us that even wise, talented, courageous, and compassionate individuals are fallible. They will have biases. They will lack certain skills. They will make mistakes. They, like all of us, are products of their culture and generation, unintentionally or willfully blind to the ways in which the status quo hurts others. They, and the organizations and movements they've developed, will always be flawed.

Just as sensitives want to idealize a cause, we will be tempted to idealize individuals, groups, and organizations. We may read a leader's book or hear a team member speak or learn about an organization's mission and believe that we have just discovered the most wonderful, inspirational people on the planet. Such idealism, while energizing, can lead to despair if we don't learn to temper our expectations and accept the human limitations we each carry.

It's important to approach any group, organization, or movement with our eyes wide open, asking questions—first, of ourselves and where our own tolerance levels are. *What behaviors, fallibilities, or shortcomings can I live with, and what is too upsetting or triggering for me? If I have clients or particular populations I am serving, can I manage those interactions without becoming overwhelmed? How many people is too many people when it comes to regular contact and collaboration?*

It's also essential to ask questions of the people we may be working with, through informal conversations or formal interviews, to learn more about them and how they operate. *What is your managerial style? How do you respond to the pressures of the work? What do teamwork and collaboration look like in your organization? How do you support and encourage one another?* What you learn in response to these questions can play a major role in determining if an organization, group, or activity is right for you.

Emotional labor is a term coined by sociologist Arlie Hochschild to describe the process of managing your emotions and expressions to fulfill the requirements of a job.[18] Also called *emotion work* or *emotion management*, this concept recognizes the effort and energy required for, say, a restaurant server to remain pleasant and polite even when a customer is being rude. Any role that involves direct contact with members of the public or tries to elicit an emotional response from someone else (e.g., inspiring people to donate or sign a petition) involves a level of emotional labor.

Nearly everyone working in social justice will need to engage in emotional labor. The issues we confront are so challenging, the injustices so terrible, and the suffering so awful that we probably all have moments when we want to scream or weep or curl into a ball. But there aren't many places, especially within professional organizations, where those kinds of emotional responses are welcome. We need to hold it in to some extent, especially if we want to build a career or influence others to join or support a cause.

The effort to regulate emotions while doing such emotional work would be significant for anyone, but for feelings-driven individuals, the energy required is even greater. This is another reason why the people you interact with in the course of your social justice activities are so important. Perhaps you need to be careful about expressing your emotions with the general public or community leaders and elected officials, but what about your colleagues? Your supervisor? Do they give you space to express your true emotions, or do you have to hide it from them as well? How much time do you spend with people who require you to manage your emotions, compared to times when you can express yourself more fully? Staying in a position where you have to be "incongruent," where what you're feeling is different from the emotions you're allowed to express, "is stressful and will increasingly shift you into chronic and eventually traumatic stress," explains Barrie Jaeger.[19] But working with and around people who are supportive and authentic can bring greater joy to your efforts, amplify your courage, and sustain you for the longer term.

I think of Melba Beals, one of the Little Rock Nine who helped integrate an Arkansas high school in 1957. At first glance, Beals did not seem like the ideal candidate for such an important, dangerous mission. She absorbed the palpable fear of her parents and grandparents in segregated Little Rock and grew up terrified of anyone with white skin and blue eyes. She was so scared that "when my blue-eyed cousins came to babysit us, I hid in the closet or under a bed."[20]

Yet at only fifteen years of age, she volunteered to go to Central High School as one of its first Black students. I believe it's no coincidence that Beals had a close and supportive family who taught her self-confidence and self-love. She carried a steel-sure faith in God, thanks in large part to her grandmother. She also had the backing of the school board and the NAACP, who collaborated closely on the logistics of bringing the nine students into the school. She received encouraging visits from Dr. King and other civil rights leaders. And as the death threats became more serious and the segregationist mobs became more violent, she and her peers eventually had the protection of the Little Rock police force and 101st Airborne Division soldiers.

With a community of supporters, defenders, and protectors around her, Beals endured an entire school year of harassment, bullying, verbal and physical assaults, death threats, isolation and lockdowns for her protection—as well as the loss of her beloved grandmother to leukemia—before moving to California to finish her education. She could be so resilient because she knew who she was; she knew what she was called to do and why it mattered; and she was buoyed by a host of supporters who stayed with her through an incredibly scary experience. Bolstered by the love, encouragement, and protection of many, Beals was able to play a pivotal role in rewriting history.

Who knows what you could do if you found the right people to do it with? When we have a strong team or community around us, we can absorb their strength, courage, and hope when we don't have enough of our own. We can share our deepest fears and doubts in safety; we can learn from their wisdom and skills. Yes, they will be imperfect, and there will probably be disagreements. But if you can create an authentic, supportive space together, if you can work through conflict with respect and empathy, your collective potential to serve the greater good in a meaningful and sustainable way is far greater. You may even find yourself doing things you never could on your own, taking on seemingly impossible problems with an incredible team of kind and dedicated individuals.

We need one another. We are better with one another. And that's when change can begin.

***Who* questions to consider:**

- Who is a social justice leader (past or present) that I admire? What are this person's strengths and flaws?
- Who is someone that I have really enjoyed collaborating with? What about this person made it a positive experience?

- What type of people do I tend to get along well with?
- What type of people do I have the most conflict with, or that cause me the most stress?
- What type of people do I want to learn from?
- Are there specific behaviors, attitudes, and personalities that are too triggering for me?
- How well do I manage conflict? Are there conflict management or conflict resolution skills that I would like to learn?
- How many people can I comfortably interact with on a day-to-day basis? How many people is it a stretch for me to interact with daily? How many people is absolutely too many?
- What kind of support, affirmation, and encouragement would it be most helpful for me to receive from my social justice colleagues? From my supervisor?
- How much effort does it take for me to manage my emotions around other people?
- In any given day, what is my ideal mix of alone time and time with people? How about over the course of a week?
- Who is someone I can call on when I'm feeling overwhelmed, need support, or need to vent?
- Who do I know who could mentor me on my social justice journey?

9

When

The Long Arc of Justice in Our Own Lives

"Do not fear going forward slowly;
fear only to stand still."
Chinese proverb

On March 14, 1977, in a Monday homily in his church in San Salvador, El Salvador, Archbishop Óscar Romero said, "We will be firm in defending our rights—but with a great love in our hearts."[1]

Just two days earlier, Romero's good friend and Jesuit priest Rutilio Grande García had been assassinated by government security forces after condemning government-sanctioned violence against the poor in El Salvador. Low-income families had few rights and resources against the military-dominated government and the wealthy. Among his many different efforts, Grande organized marginalized rural farmers in El Salvador to demand land reform and justice. "Rutilio's parish at Aguilares was a very important center of this work for justice," Jesuit priest and biographer Rodolfo Cardenal later wrote. "[The ruling classes] knew he was a leader and they decided to kill him."[2]

For more than thirty years, Óscar Romero had faithfully served as a priest in several different cities in El Salvador. But he did not challenge the oppressive policies of the government. He did not advocate or speak out for the marginalized, or support other priests who did. In fact, when Romero was first appointed Archbishop of San Salvador in February 1977, only seventeen days before Rutilio Grande's murder, government officials supported his promotion. His fellow priests did not.[3]

But then Father Grande was machine-gunned to death, along with an elderly gentleman and a young boy from Grande's parish, by a right-wing government death squad. Seemingly overnight, the fifty-nine-year-old Óscar Romero transformed from a quiet observer on the sidelines into El Salvador's loudest, clearest voice for justice, equity, and peace.

"When I looked at Rutilio lying there dead I thought, 'If they have killed him for doing what he did, then I too have to walk the same path,'" Romero later reflected.[4] His time to act had arrived.

We often think of social justice activists as young and in the prime of life—idealistic, energetic, and unencumbered. Martin Luther King was only twenty-six when he led the Montgomery Bus Boycott. The Student Nonviolent Coordinating Committee (SNCC), led by college students, was one of the most influential organizations of the civil rights movement. The anti-war movement of 1965–73 was largely driven by students and young adults.[5] From the streets of Johannesburg during apartheid to Tiananmen Square in 1989, from Occupy Wall Street to the 2021 climate change protests in Glasgow, Scotland, young people have been at the heart of many of the most powerful collective actions of the last century.

But that is only one part of the story of social movements, which have been led, inspired, and organized by individuals in nearly every stage of life. Cesar Chavez was thirty-eight when the Delano Grape Strike first began. Mother Teresa was forty years old when she founded the Missionaries of Charity. Mahatma Gandhi returned to India to begin his organizing work when he was forty-five. Henri Nouwen was fifty-four when he left behind a long, distinguished career in academia and the clergy to dedicate his efforts to serving people with developmental disabilities. Alicia Zubasnabar de la Cuadra, whose husband and children were kidnapped and eventually murdered by the 1970s military dictatorship in Argentina, began protesting the widespread kidnappings of young children when she was sixty-two years old, eventually cofounding the activist organization Abuelas de la Plaza de Mayo (Grandmothers of the Plaza de Mayo).[6] Individuals in their seventies, eighties, and beyond are today engaging in efforts to address climate change, women's rights, voting rights, and more. The list of change agents who have made their mark on our societies cuts across every age and generation. The call to justice can open hearts and propel action at any life stage.

The question of *when* to engage in social justice work is a highly personal one, and the response will be different for everyone. But for no one should the response be "always." For activists to remain healthy and resilient, they require regular times of rest and reconnection with themselves, their loved ones, and nature. This might come through dedicated hours here and there—or it could come through long seasons focused on inner work, healing, learning, and other meaningful activities. There may be times in our lives when being an activist is simply not possible, as when we are caring for sick family members or raising young children or facing significant challenges in our lives.

Parenting, for example, is more taxing for sensitive individuals than their nonsensitive peers. Sensitive parents report becoming more overwhelmed and having to rely on less effective parenting methods as a result.[7] This doesn't mean sensitive and empathic individuals aren't great parents. With their ability to intuit and connect with their children's needs, they often are. But intensive caretaking of small humans takes a lot of energy out of the sensitive soul, and will likely leave limited emotional resources for other heart-heavy activities.

Since the birth of my first child, at least half of my emotional resources have been permanently set aside for my children. This has significantly transformed both the kind of social justice work I'm able to do and the level at which I can engage. But becoming a parent has also prompted deep reflection and growth. I have learned profound lessons about my own strengths and limitations, rediscovered play and childlike joy, extended my timeline of concern further into the future, and empathized more with the needs of parents and children around me.

There is no wasted time or experience in our lives; it all contributes to the development of our spirit and character, our knowledge and skills, and that, in turn, influences our ability to lead and inspire and connect. If you need to be on the sidelines for a few months, years, or even decades, honor that. There is no shame or weakness in healthy choices like that. Even when directed toward the noblest of causes, the human heart, mind, and body are not machines. Spending time focused on your own needs as a human being is extraordinarily valuable. The world will benefit from having you be the most grounded, well-rounded, and mature version of yourself you can be.

Archbishop Romero spent more than three decades as a priest serving primarily within the four walls of the church. His time as an outspoken advocate for the poor, disenfranchised, and oppressed was a very short three years before he too was tragically assassinated. But in that short time, Romero became an authoritative voice for the majority of Salvadorans, condemning the dictatorship of Gen. Carlos Humberto Romero as well as the military junta that deposed him, defending the rights of the poor and marginalized, and naming on national radio the atrocities committed against ordinary citizens.[8]

His impact was only enhanced by the maturity, influence, wisdom, and experience he had gained over his long career. He spoke with the skill of a well-practiced orator but also with the humility of someone who had taken his time to learn and understand. He took action strategically but also loved with the heart of someone who knew how to authentically connect with people. Romero's three decades in the priesthood formed him into the activist his country needed in that particular moment in history.

The question of *when* is not one we ask only once but one we revisit again and again. I have most often asked questions about timing when I have felt restless and dissatisfied, angry and aggrieved, or overwhelmed and exhausted. The issue of timing has taken precedence over other questions when I have been most in need of change. And depending on my circumstances, I have asked the question in a slightly different way:

When should I step into the arena?
When do I need to step back?
When should I move to a different organization or focus on a different issue?
When should I increase engagement or decrease involvement?
When should I take on leadership and when should I stay behind the scenes?
When do I need to focus on something else?

Our responses to *when* questions will likely change as life circumstances evolve, as various social issues come to the fore, or as opportunities open up or shut down. Being able to change direction according to our current context demonstrates a high degree of self-awareness, adaptability, and discernment.

At various times in my life, I have answered those questions based on health, finances, family needs, passions and interests, emotional limitations, and current events. And as with anything we practice, I've gotten a bit better at understanding what I need and want the more I listen to my mind and body.

The activist who balances social justice with other responsibilities and opportunities may find their timeline of engagement to be uneven and spotty. It may or may not be an ever-rising slope of greater involvement, leadership, and impact. It may wax and wane, dip and rise, shimmer and fade. Moving in and out of social activism over the course of your life is perfectly normal, and does not need to be a cause of concern. If your heartstrings are tied to the social good, you will eventually find your way back—though perhaps in a different incarnation. Our individual purposes and callings are ever-shifting and multifaceted, and our circles of concern will naturally shrink or expand in response. Many notable activists before us have lived such lives.

One of those activists is humanitarian Dorothea Lynde Dix, who became an educator at the age of nineteen, perhaps because it was one of the only professions available to women in 1821. She spent fifteen years, off and on, running her own school for girls in Boston, taking time off as needed to recover from frequent illnesses. By 1836, Dix was burned out and depressed, and her physical health had declined significantly. She closed her school and spent nearly two years abroad in England to rest and recover. There is no clear record of significant social involvement by Dix again until 1841, after she had inherited a substantial sum of money from her grandmother and could volunteer teaching Sunday school classes at the East Cambridge House of Correction in Massachusetts.

There, she found that individuals living with mental health challenges were being treated inhumanely and housed in appalling conditions—oftentimes naked, in darkness, and chained to walls. Profoundly troubled by what she witnessed, Dix was determined to foment change. She spent two years traveling and observing conditions in other institutions, after which she advocated for legislation in Massachusetts to provide more services to those with mental health disorders. She then spent the next forty years advocating for more humane treatment for people living with mental illnesses and incarcerated across the United States and Canada—but with multiple breaks to recover from her own illness, including a three-year tour of Europe when she was in her early fifties.[9]

Dix honored her limitations, both in giving herself regular time to convalesce and in focusing her energies on the one social issue she most cared about. She has been criticized for not being involved in the concurrent women's rights or abolitionist movements, but that would have taken her focus away from mental health patients. Historians speculate that Dix's own struggles with depression and poor health led her to empathize deeply with those in institutions that didn't support their well-being. She shared their pain, but as a woman of means who had experienced life outside the confines of those institutions, she recognized that mental health patients deserved dignifying care and a place in society.

The timeline of Dix's social activism, in which she became more engaged as she got older, points to another phenomenon consistently supported by psychological research: some of the more challenging aspects of being highly sensitive may diminish as we age. A 2019 study of nearly two thousand Japanese adults, for example, found a linear decline in the traits of low sensory threshold and ease of excitation (both measures of becoming easily overwhelmed) in older participants up to the age of sixty-nine. The study also found that participants' aesthetic sensitivity, or their ability to appreciate beauty and connect spiritually, actually increased with age.[10] Another large-scale study, this one in the United States, showed that people become less attuned to emotional cues and facial expressions for anger as they get older. Their ability to recognize cues signaling happiness, however, held steady regardless of age.[11]

As we get older, our brains adapt to provide us the gift of not caring or noticing as much what other people may be thinking or feeling. We aren't as bogged down with meeting others' expectations. We become a bit better at focusing on what's important and dismissing what's not. We become more attuned to the good, the beautiful, and the joyful.

With each new decade I've entered, I've felt the shift—and it is extraordinarily liberating. It's the same freedom, I imagine, that helped Óscar Romero speak so powerfully after thirty years of quiet or that gave Dorothea Dix the wherewithal to challenge legislators even as she struggled with chronic illness. Today, I can have conversations, receive feedback, and participate in events that twenty years ago would have been overwhelming. Taking things far less personally, experiencing less hurt, and more easily forgetting negative experiences come as welcome benefits of moving into later seasons of life.

For sensitive activists, this may be helpful to consider. Sometimes, the answer to the question of *when* may very legitimately be "later"—despite the sense of urgency that seems to infuse every social movement. You are not required to act according to someone else's sense of urgency. The job, volunteer role, or collective action that is too overwhelming for you now may be something you can do in the future. The person, group, or issue you're not ready to confront now may feel less intimidating as you age and mature. And remember: any time you spend now focusing on your education or career, or financially supporting your family, or caring for loved ones is valuable and meaningful, ethical and just—and part of shaping how you contribute to the social good in the future.

Of course, let's not forget that youth comes with its own gifts: namely, more energy and strength, a higher tolerance for audio and visual stimuli, and a greater ability to filter out less important sensory input.[12] Attending a protest or rally, participating in large events, or working in noisy, visually stimulating environments is generally easier for younger individuals.

Young people also typically have fewer emotionally demanding responsibilities than their older counterparts.

The timing of your engagement with social activism is yours to decide. There is no one answer. There is no right answer. You have the opportunity to build your own unique timeline, one that progresses and pauses as you need it to. And as we incorporate the regular rhythm of considering *when* into our lives, we will become all the wiser and more aware of our place in the long arc of the moral universe.

The activist stage need not belong only to the young or even the young at heart. The world needs young spirits, old souls, and everyone in between to contribute what they are able to *when* they are able to. Whenever you have the time, the energy, the wisdom, and the inspiration to join the effort, there will be a place for you.

***When* questions to consider:**

- How old are (or were) the activists and social justice heroes I admire when they were most active? How do I see them leveraging their age in their work?
- What is my current life stage? What advantages do I have in this stage? What limitations?
- When do I find time to take care of my body, mind, and spirit? Do I need more time, or is this sufficient?
- Is the current amount of time I'm putting toward social justice satisfying to me? If not, why not?
- When will there be a major transition coming up in my life? How might that affect my level of engagement?
- What are the greatest responsibilities I have toward myself, my family, and others in my community right now? How much of my time and energy do those responsibilities require?
- What are the telltale signs (physical, emotional, circumstantial, etc.) that I need to get more involved in social justice?

- What are the typical signs from my mind, body, and spirit that I need to reduce my involvement or pause it altogether?
- At what life stage will social justice work be hard to fit into my life? When will there be more space for it?
- What traits or skills am I hoping to develop as I age?
- What kind of activism does it make sense to do later in life?

10
Where

The Places and Spaces That Help Us Thrive

"Be sure you put your feet in the right place. Then stand firm."

Abraham Lincoln

"What is the most powerful force in the world?"

Bill Drayton asked himself this question while spending the summer in India after his first year of college. He and three friends had spent days interviewing shopkeepers and villagers, trying to understand the country's economic and political systems, and imagining possible solutions that could raise the standard of living for Indian families to match the standard for American families.

Drayton's conclusion? The most powerful force in the world is "always a big idea, but only if it's in the hands of a truly great entrepreneur."[1] After finishing his studies, Drayton served in the Environmental Protection Agency for a time and then founded an organization called Ashoka. He hoped to nurture, equip, and empower what he called *social entrepreneurs*—businesspeople leading for-profit companies that create social good. They may fill gaps in the market that more traditional businesses can't fill; they may innovate new product solutions that NGOs and government agencies aren't equipped to do; they may pioneer new service models that are more efficient and self-sustaining. Since 1981, Ashoka has selected more than four thousand social entrepreneurs from over ninety countries for their fellowship program, providing them with funding, training, and networks.[2]

Drayton's vision for harnessing the innovation, adaptability, and ambition of business toward solving social challenges has fueled a passionate movement in the decades since. Ashoka is now just one actor in an ever-broadening field of organizations, networks, investment funds, and business schools that are supporting social entrepreneurs in hopes that they will have the next great idea for solving the world's most intractable problems.

Social enterprises today are actively involved in addressing healthcare disparities, information access, energy poverty, financial access, women's empowerment, the technology gap, climate change, and much more. While it's hard to say how many social enterprises—also called *social impact businesses*—exist today, this statistic indicates how powerfully the notion of leveraging business for social change has taken hold: The European Commission of the European Union has reported that one out of every four new enterprises set up there each year is a social enterprise.[3]

What brought us to China was a social enterprise, cofounded by my husband. I had sworn off for-profit companies after college, choosing to work in pretty much every other type of organization: grassroots nonprofits, foundations, faith-based organizations, and government agencies. But the potential for large-scale impact in a socially driven, investor-backed business was too alluring even for me, so I gladly joined Ned's business when we moved overseas.

The work was indeed incredibly impactful. But it was also far more stressful than any of my previous jobs. I felt this constant push for *more*: shorter deadlines, faster turnarounds, higher returns, more sales. The work was endless and the pressure never let up—which, as I mentioned earlier, eventually led to my soul-wrenching burnout.

A start-up, it turns out, was not a good place for me. But what doesn't work for me may be perfect for you. The social enterprise sector, and business in general, could benefit from more workers and leaders who are thoughtful, compassionate, and empathic. According to Deloitte research, businesses around the world are increasingly interested in inclusion, citizenship, social impact, and employee well-being. But across retailers and hedge funds, hospitality companies and tech firms, too few executives understand these trends and so are unable to collaboratively lead their teams in these areas.[4] Imagine how profoundly our societies could be transformed if the business sector were heavily influenced by people committed to kindness, fairness, and equity.

Just as social change can come through a broad range of personalities, it can also be facilitated through a broad range of organizations, from a one-person agency or small band of volunteers to a government department or multinational organization. In a *New York Times*–compiled list of the most significant moments in the American disability rights movement, progress took place through Congress; rehabilitation centers; college campuses; record labels that featured artists with disabilities like Ray Charles and Stevie Wonder; television shows like *Sesame Street*; news agencies; the Food and Drug Administration; federal lawsuits; sit-in and "lie-down" protests; international conferences; grassroots organizations; the Supreme Court; parades; academic research; and national nonprofits.[5] It takes not just a village but an entire ecosystem of individuals, groups, nonprofits, businesses, institutions, and government agencies to make our communities more just.

The question of *where* to invest your passions and skills is especially important for sensitive individuals, as we are deeply affected by our physical environments—from the lights and sounds, to the decor and ambience, to the conversations and moods of other people. If this is where you will spend a significant amount of time doing work that is already emotionally stretching, it is perfectly reasonable to seek an environment that does not add to your stress. It makes sense to try to avoid the workplace pitfalls that, according to sociologists, most often lead to burnout: "overload, lack of control, lack of rewards, lack of community, lack of fairness, and strong value conflicts."[6]

Most social justice roles require us to be in multiple physical environments. Three key environments are (1) the physical space where you will spend the most time working; (2) the group or organization you choose to be a part of; and (3) the broader environment in which that organization operates, including the community, neighborhood, region, and country. The path toward justice, the activities along the way, and your experience of them will be heavily influenced by these environments. For example, a march for LGBTQ rights with music and dancing and inspirational speakers in a safe and welcoming location will be an entirely different experience from an LGBTQ march that traverses through hostile communities and actively engages with counterprotesters or security forces. Or the efforts of a small group of immigrants advocating for education access in their home country will feel almost nothing like the program of a multinational NGO trying to secure education opportunities in that same country.

Fortunately, it's possible to get a good sense of an environment with a bit of investigation. Your physical working space is the most straightforward. If you are working for an organization, try to visit it before making any commitments. Take some time to assess what your sensory experience of the space would be—the level and type of light, the noises, the smells, and the textures. You can ask to see your future workstation or one like it, and find out what allowances the organization makes for accessibility, ergonomics, and decor. Or if you are working from home, make sure your dedicated workspace is set up well for comfort and productivity. Even small adaptations in your physical workspace can help prevent unpleasant sensory stimulation, allowing you to focus your energy on your work rather than external distractions.

Groups and organizations are more complicated. Every organization has its own characteristics—its own ways of talking and behaving and making decisions. Every group has a different approach to activism, collaboration, and community engagement. These are all elements that make up what social scientists call *organizational culture.*

No matter its size or sector, an organization's culture infuses almost every aspect of how people within the organization work together, treat one another, and prioritize their activities. Brand expert and author Denise Lee Yohn defines *organizational culture* as "the ways people in the organization behave and the attitudes and beliefs that inform those behaviors (i.e., 'the way we do things around here')—including formal, stated norms as well as implicit ways people work and interact."[7] An organization's culture is shaped by dozens of factors, including its leaders, stated mission, goals, values, history, projects, resources, legacy, members, public perception, and broader place in history and culture.

Some organizations intentionally set about developing and maintaining an internal culture; others have a more organic approach, letting the culture grow on its own. But even small, informal groups have a culture, whether they are aware of it or not. Understanding that culture will help you figure out if you would feel welcomed in that space. Looking at culture will also help you assess if an organization actually embodies its mission and values in its daily operations. Sensitive individuals are especially attuned to noticing inconsistencies, which could lead to significant frustration and stress. As you try to deduce the nature of an organization's culture, questions to explore include:

How do group members treat one another?
How is conflict resolved?
Are "quieter" people given space to speak up and lead?
Does the organization genuinely care about activists' well-being instead of promoting martyrdom for the cause?

Unfortunately, it's not uncommon for the officially recognized culture to differ from what happens on the ground. Or for the actual experience of the culture to differ from what the leaders want it to be. "At many organizations," Yohn explains, "there is a gap between the existing culture and the 'desired' culture—the culture needed to support and advance the company's goals and strategies."[8] In this case, deeper investigation may be required. If you're interviewing for a paid position, come prepared with questions to help you assess the organizational culture. If you're signing up to be a volunteer, have an in-depth conversation with your supervisor or fellow volunteers before committing. Former employees and former volunteers can also be treasure troves of helpful information; for the most part, they don't have an agenda and are free to share the totality of their experience. In addition, listen to your intuition. In all likelihood, you'll sense what the organizational culture is like simply by being in the environment and observing how people interact with one another.

While every organization is unique, there are some general but major cultural differences between for-profit companies, nonprofits, and government agencies. No sector perfectly operates or optimally takes care of its people, but all have something to offer their staff and volunteers, as well as the community at large. As you consider organizations, it will be helpful to have a sense of what you need in an organizational culture in order to thrive, what would be nice to have, and what you cannot tolerate. Let's take a look at some of the key drivers of each sector's organizational culture.

For-profit companies tend to emphasize innovation, adaptability, and growth—values that create fast-paced, high-energy environments. They may offer plenty of opportunities for professional development and learning valuable skills. But being part of a business, even one with a strong social mission, requires being able to operate within the norms, practices, and social networks of the business sector. This may include a greater emphasis on quantitative outputs: contacts, sales, customers, revenue, and more. It may require close adherence to maintaining a corporate image or satisfying investors. When assessing social enterprises, it's critical to determine how their social mission is weighted in comparison to these other potentially competing interests. If they had to choose one and sacrifice the other, which would be prioritized?

Large nonprofits and foundations can feel somewhat like businesses because they are also concerned about funding, image, and returns. Instead of investors, large nonprofits need to please donors and funders. They tend to invest significant resources in growing their donor base and maintaining their well-funded programs. There is far less opportunity for innovation, but they can very effectively serve large numbers of people in their areas of expertise. Most of them are relatively stable and well positioned to respond to the needs of society. But they can feel bureaucratic and inefficient. With larger nonprofits, a key question to ask is: How are they balancing the needs of the community with the needs of donors?

Small nonprofits, especially grassroots nonprofits, are very people-driven. Every person on the team matters; most people wear multiple hats; close collaboration and teamwork is a necessity rather than a choice. There are huge opportunities for learning and growth, as well as room for creativity and innovation. But the amount of work can be overwhelming, and the pressure to maintain sustainable sources of funding rarely lets up. Working for a small nonprofit usually means living with the ongoing risk of having your salary cut or losing your job altogether. When I look at small nonprofits, I often wonder: Are they able to think strategically in terms of what is sustainable for the organization and its people, or are they more focused on survival?

Government agencies touch almost all aspects of our lives, providing far-reaching opportunities to promote equity and human rights. It can be easy to forget that government agencies can also be instigators of social change, not just the target of social change movements. Even one individual in a key position can catalyze societal-level transformation. For example, when Danny Ortega Jr. was chairman of the Arizona Industrial Commission in the 1970s, he led efforts to ban the short-handled hoe, a tool used by migrant farmworkers that "caused ruptured spinal disks, arthritis, and other serious back injuries."[9] He rallied his colleagues to institute a new regulation banning the hoe by a vote of 5 to 0, saving thousands of people from a lifetime of debilitating pain.

Government agencies have power, influence, and resources. But public institutions can also be old behemoths, resistant to change. Programs may be implemented more by rote than anything else. When looking at opportunities within the public sector, an important consideration is: Are there any peers or leaders who are motivated to undergo the sometimes herculean effort to make necessary changes to continue to serve effectively?

Unsurprisingly, a fair number of sensitives prefer to work on their own, operating as entrepreneurs, consultants, free agents, or a one-person shop. There may be times in your life when it makes perfect sense to work alone. But don't forget that HSPs and empaths often benefit from being out in the world, interacting with others and stretching ourselves, in order to stay healthy and ensure that our sensitivities don't overwhelm us. Even when working on your own, it's a good idea to find ways to interact and partner with others. Doing so will nurture your mental health and amplify your effectiveness.

No matter where you end up—in a business, nonprofit, informal group, or on your own—there will also be a larger context to consider. This broader environment will influence the organization and you. Is it a neighborhood and community that is comfortable for you, or one that will challenge you? How much energy will you need to expend to understand the language, culture, and norms of the surrounding community? Do you feel safe there, or are there risks to your physical and emotional well-being?

In the early days of my career, I thought it was the height of nobility to live *and* work in the most challenging of neighborhoods. I wanted to be able to live in a slum or a hut, easily dismissing the lack of conveniences because my life was so rich in purpose and community. I wanted to be like Mother Teresa (minus the nun part)—being among the marginalized and underserved, doing meaningful service, and living the ultimate life of contentment and meaning.

But that is only the myth of Mother Teresa. As revealed in private letters to confidantes and mentors released after her death, Mother Teresa wrestled with severe depression and lackluster faith for almost the entirety of the fifty years she spent serving in India. "So many unanswered questions live within me afraid to uncover them. . . . Did I make a mistake in surrendering blindly to the Call of the Sacred Heart?" she wrote at one point.[10]

I don't admire Mother Teresa any less for her questions and doubts. In fact, I have a greater regard for her perseverance and commitment in the face of depression and struggle. But even for her, living and working in an environment filled with mass poverty, illness, and suffering was *hard.* If you choose to do this, it may wound your spirit and cause you immeasurable grief. Is this a burden you want to carry, on top of your desire to make this a brighter and better world? I know I'm not able to, but perhaps you can. Your caring, empathic presence in a community that is suffering could be a significant gift to others.

The environments we place ourselves in can have a profound effect on our mental, emotional, and physical health. Whether cubicles or living rooms, office buildings or entire neighborhoods, these are not environments in which we simply exist. We absorb their energy and culture, and carry that with us. What physical spaces, organizations, and communities will best nurture your efforts toward social progress? Figuring out the best fit for you may require investigation and experimentation, conversation and reflection, mistakes and failures, but as long as you keep looking, you will get there—wherever that may be.

***Where* questions to consider:**

- What do I need in my workspace to feel focused, productive, and comfortable?
- Where can I go when I want to relax, unplug, and recover from the stresses of my day?
- What things in my environment particularly bother my senses (sights, smells, sounds, etc.)? Is it possible to avoid these in my work environment?
- What types of organizational cultures have I encountered—in school, at work, or in the community? What in those cultures have I enjoyed? What has been hard for me to manage?
- Of the different types of organizations listed in this chapter, which ones seem like they might be a good fit? Which ones do I want to learn more about? Are there ones I should probably avoid?
- What attributes of an organization help me to feel especially engaged? Innovation or consistency? Teamwork or independent work? Broad impact or deep, focused impact? Full of activity or quiet? Leader-driven

or consensus-driven? Emphasis on qualitative work or quantitative work?

- Is there an organization or group I can visit to learn more about their workspace and culture?
- If I am considering a specific role, who can I ask to learn more about the culture of the group or organization?
- How important is job security or financial security to me?
- How important are opportunities for promotion or career growth?
- What do I need in my place of work and residence to feel emotionally and physically safe?
- In my current community of residence (neighborhood, city, country), what feeds my soul? What exhausts me or stresses me out?
- If I had to be stretched either in my place of work or in my area of residence, where would I prefer to be stretched? Where would I rather not be stretched?

Part III

Pathways and Possibilities

11

Your Imagination Unleashed

"Man cannot discover new oceans unless he
has the courage to lose sight of the shore."
Ándre Gide

What if I told you that Christmas lights, soccer balls, and handwritten notes stopped a decades-long war?

On the face of it, it sounds like an irrational and implausible combination of approaches for effecting change. It doesn't fit with what we understand to be effective peacemaking or social activism. It doesn't match the patterns and categories of justice work that we hold in our heads.

"The human brain is a pattern-matching machine," explains journalist and author Tom Vanderbilt. "Categories help us manage the torrent of information we receive and sort the world into easier-to-read patterns."[1]

The ability to categorize is extraordinarily useful for humans. It provides us with a clear answer to important questions like: *Is this a threat? Should I move toward or away? Will this help or hurt me?* And when we can't categorize something—say, a song that doesn't fit a particular genre—we feel uneasy. We are far more likely to decide that we don't like a song if we can't give it a clear label.

The same holds true for social justice activism. We *know* the categories of protest organizers, speakers, marchers, petitioners, canvassers, and outspoken critics. We've seen the movies and read the books, and these kinds of figures are the ones we see featured over and over again: The activist lawyer. The progressive politician. The inspiring orator. The dogged petitioner. The courageous interventionist. The relentless protester. The public debater. The charismatic movement leader.

This, to us, is the work of social justice. If someone is doing something entirely different, yet still claims to be an activist, we are skeptical. We are wired to want to fit everyone—including ourselves—into the well-known grooves of long-held categories. If someone doesn't fit, we are forced to grapple with tension, with dissonance. And that is a very uncomfortable place to be.

Highly sensitive individuals have a particular knack for spotting what is different and what doesn't fit. We see the details that diverge; we notice what's breaking well-organized patterns. We are very aware if *we* are the ones who aren't fitting in, and that knowledge will likely make us anxious, fearful, and stressed.

This, perhaps more than anything else, is the challenge of social justice for the sensitive soul: imagining a different way of serving the social good, one that is uniquely tailored to who we are in the world. You could spend all the time you want reflecting, making lists, taking personality tests, and checking boxes. You could know yourself—your interests, gifts, traits, passions, limitations, and needs—inside out. But can you take all that self-knowledge and information, and create a new vision for yourself? Do you have the courage to break the mold and be confident that what you are doing is meaningful and worthwhile, even if others aren't able to?

Discovering your own social justice niche may require breaking well-established categories and jettisoning long-held assumptions. Like trail builders who create hiking paths through the wilderness, making our way requires moving aside brush and bramble, rocks and branches, that might prevent us from generating a path forward. Those around us may be confused, uncomfortable, or even resentful when we choose to build our own trails rather than traveling their well-worn ones. But they're not necessarily in the right. The categories and assumptions of the activist world are imperfect to begin with; for too many of us, they limit our imaginations and paradigms for how social change can happen.

Will we allow ourselves the creative license to seek a different path? According to researcher Kyung Hee Kim, our creativity declines as we age because we get bogged down by the idea that there are right answers and wrong answers.[2] It's not that our creativity dissipates or our imaginations shrink; rather, we simply stop permitting ourselves to come up with unusual, norm-busting ideas. Like any skill, our creativity can get rusty if we don't use it regularly. But if nurtured and encouraged, creativity can flourish at any age.

Creativity is one of humanity's most powerful tools in the fight against inequality and oppression. If the solutions being pursued today were wholly effective, humanity's long-standing injustices would have been resolved long ago. Clearly, there is room for improvement. There is room for doing things differently. There is room for new possibilities, wild ideas, and unheard-of strategies. Who knows? They might be exactly what is needed—just like Christmas lights, soccer balls, and handwritten notes.

The Colombian military did not rely on the usual strategies when they needed help ending the conflict against guerrilla forces, especially the Revolutionary Armed Forces of Colombia (FARC), at the beginning of the twenty-first century. They had been fighting the insurgents for more than forty years, and despite significant headway, the country's leaders realized that military solutions alone would not dissolve the rebel groups or stop the violence.

So, beginning in 2006, military personnel turned to an unexpected source for help: Bogotá-based executive Jose Miguel Sokoloff, considered one of the best advertising minds in the world. The Colombian military needed to convince the remaining guerrillas to voluntarily give up their arms, and they needed to convince communities to embrace the guerrillas after so many years of violence. Who better to do this than an expert in advertising, who had spent years influencing the decisions and behaviors of others?

Sokoloff and his team began with ad campaigns and television commercials that aired regularly across the country. In 2010, they launched what they called Operation Christmas. They wanted to leverage the holiday to encourage the guerrillas, hidden deep in the jungles, to come home. That year, they set up motion-sensor Christmas lights on nine 75-foot trees deep in rebel territory. Whenever someone walked by, the lights would turn on, illuminating a banner that read: "If Christmas can come to the jungle, you can come home. Demobilize. At Christmas, everything is possible." About 330 guerrillas, or 5 percent of the FARC force, actually responded, coming out of the jungle and giving themselves up.

The next Christmas, they sent lighted messages and gifts—from ordinary citizens and even from Colombia's president—down the rivers into the jungle. More guerrillas came home. Sokoloff, in ongoing close coordination with the military, played recorded messages from ex-guerrillas and the mothers of rebels on speaker systems; they provided beams of lights in villages to show guerrillas the way home; they asked football players, celebrities, and ordinary citizens to sign thousands of soccer balls, and threw them out of helicopters across rebel-held territory. Each ball was emblazoned with a sticker that said, "Demobilize. Let's play again."[3]

Over the course of eight years, eighteen thousand rebels put down their arms. The FARC finally agreed to negotiate with the Colombian government beginning in 2012. A cease-fire was signed in 2016. And Colombia, once one of the most violent countries in the world, is now relatively peaceful and is making progress in stabilizing its economy and defending human rights.[4]

Sokoloff and his unconventional advertising campaigns are credited with playing a major role in ending nearly fifty years of violence and terrorism in Colombia. While an offbeat form of activism, the demobilization advertising campaign actually incorporated several key elements of successful social movements: It was nonviolent. It promoted empathy on both sides of the conflict. It engaged the broader citizenry in simple and meaningful ways. It had a clear, attainable goal. And it harnessed the best creative minds in Colombia toward doing something that had never been done before.

These are the kinds of ideas that our world needs more of—ideas that are full of peace, empathy, hope, and beauty. But first, we need people who can dream those ideas, who can unleash their imagination in new and exciting directions for the good of humanity. We need people who are willing to help redefine what social justice work looks like and reshape who social activists are.

At the beginning of their advertising campaign, I'm guessing no one—not Sokoloff, the military leaders, or even President Juan Manuel Santos—had any idea if their unusual idea would work. They probably had plenty of doubts along the way. But they were willing to try. They were willing to fail. They were willing to persist.

This is the kind of creativity that sensitives can excel at. But we need to give ourselves permission to be creative, to not worry about getting it exactly right or fitting someone else's definitions. What you want to do may not be in an existing job description. The strategy you want to try may not even have a name. The type of organization you want to build may be a mix of different sectors that don't typically go together. Creativity requires experimentation; experimentation necessitates failure; failure pushes us to learn, iterate, and try again.

Stanford design experts Bill Burnett and Dave Evans, in their book *Designing Your Life: Build the Perfect Career, Step by Step*, compare figuring out your vocation to wayfinding. "Wayfinding is the ancient art of figuring out where you are going when you don't actually know your destination," they explain. "For wayfinding, you need a compass and you need a direction. Not a map—a direction. . . . Since there's no *one* destination in life, you can't put your goal into your GPS and get the turn-by-turn directions for how to get there. What you can do is pay attention to the clues in front of you, and make your best way forward with the tools you have at hand."[5]

You don't need to know exactly what your role should be in the world of social justice in order to engage. Or if you thought you knew, it's okay to change your mind. Most of your fellow activists haven't figured it out either. But you can still feel your way forward, bit by bit, new opportunity by new opportunity.

Dr. Izzeldin Abuelaish, a Palestinian advocate for Israeli-Palestinian peace and a fertility specialist who has worked in Israeli hospitals, uses his medical expertise to advocate for women's rights among both Arab and Jewish families. He has encouraged Palestinian medical students and doctors to do their residencies in Israeli hospitals, in hopes that greater trust and opportunities for professional collaboration can flourish. And he continues his advocacy for peace even after a 2009 Israeli air strike hit his home in the Gaza Strip and killed three of his daughters and his niece.

Dr. Abuelaish has also seen many others, both Palestinians and Israelis, expand the coalition for peace and human rights in unique ways:

> There are peace camps and summer schools and "surfers for peace" and hip-hop rappers beating out peace messages. There are endless school projects and Web sites devoted to peace, and there's even a peace phone line. . . . There are even basketball leagues for Arab-Israeli and Jewish teenagers who believe in promoting coexistence and tolerance, and an industrial project on the northern border between Israel and the West Bank whose raison d'être is coexistence. There are conferences all over the world devoted to finding a way to bring Palestinians and Israelis together.[6]

While these many efforts have not yet resulted in the widespread restoration of rights for Palestinians or sustainable peace between the two states, they are transforming individuals and families. And change at the community or national level always begins with individuals and families determined to build a more hopeful and equitable future.

In the remaining chapters of the book, we'll look at several different categories of activists who have catalyzed social change—not by marching or debating, but simply by being themselves and doing what they're good at. Within each category are multiple examples of jobs, roles, and activities that utilize traits and gifts that sensitive, empathic individuals often have. And each chapter includes real-life examples of individuals who have applied their best abilities toward expanding rights, access, and equality in less conventional—but exceedingly effective—ways.

As you read these chapters, some questions to consider include: *Could I see myself doing this? What would it be like for me to advocate for justice in this way? Which aspects of this work really appeal to me? Which do not interest me? Do I have similar skills, interests, or character traits to offer? What other possibilities come to mind?*

This is not to suggest that all sensitives and empaths should try to commit themselves to one of these areas of work. Just as you do not need to be the next Martin Luther King or Gandhi, you do not need to pursue any of these activities if they do not match who you are and what you want to do. There are many, many other options for meaningful activism outside of the ideas presented here. My hope is to simply expand our definitions of social activism, to grow our categories for justice work, and to spark our imaginations for what could be. By providing a sampling of possibilities to inspire questions and ideas, maybe your creative juices will begin to flow.

Parker Palmer writes about how, when he first wanted to dedicate himself to social change, he aimed for imitation rather than authenticity. He, like many of us, wanted to be just like his social justice heroes. Yet this approach didn't really work. "The results were rarely admirable, often laughable, and sometimes grotesque," he reflects. "But always they were unreal, a distortion of my true self—as must be the case when one lives from the outside in, not the inside out. I had simply found a 'noble' way to live a life that was not my own, a life spent imitating heroes instead of listening to my heart." The vocation that best honors our true self, according to Palmer, "comes from listening."[7]

What are your heart, mind, and body telling you? How can your love of social justice be holistically integrated with your other loves? How can you be you—wonderful, sensitive, empathic, distinct you—while working to move the needle on social change? What possibilities can you allow yourself to imagine?

It is worth reminding ourselves once again that every social movement has been populated by a wide range of personalities with an extensive variety of skills, gifts, and interests. When I first started researching this book, I was worried that it would be difficult to find inspiring social justice heroes who quietly and doggedly agitated for change, far away from the conflict and noise. Instead, I discovered too many to include in only one book. We don't typically hear about most of them, but that doesn't diminish their contributions. There would be no abolitionist movement, suffrage movement, disability rights movement, labor movement, or any other movement without the deeply passionate, beautifully creative, and wildly talented individuals who contribute in every possible sector, job, and role—out of the spotlight, behind desks and across kitchen tables, in words and numbers and images—to nudge our societies forward. We would not be able to celebrate the progress we've made without their willingness to give what they had to give.

I hope you will feel the freedom to imagine, to hope, to experiment, to break categories wide open, and to simply be. You, just as you are, are exactly what our world needs.

12

Connectors

"Justice is what love looks like in public."

Cornel West

Harvard University public policy professor Robert D. Putnam published a book in 2000 that reverberated across American communities. *Bowling Alone: The Collapse and Revival of American Community* traced an alarming downward trend in *social capital*, a term used by social scientists to refer to the "value of social networks, bonding similar people and bridging between diverse people, with norms of reciprocity."[1] Social capital, according to political scientists, is "the goodwill available to individuals or groups. Its source lies in the structure and content of the actor's social relations. Its effects flow from the information, influence, and solidarity it makes available to the actor."[2] The more social capital, the more benefits individuals and communities experience, including greater bonds of trust, an increased willingness to help one another, and a greater sense of responsibility to others.

Putnam used research into shrinking participation in all kinds of groups, organizations, and institutions that foster engagement and community—from the NAACP and unions, to church services and country clubs, to bowling leagues and marching bands—to demonstrate that our social ties are weakening or severing altogether.[3] We are becoming more distrustful and isolated. Our communities are becoming more dispersed, making it harder to develop a sense of solidarity or to organize collective actions.

More than two decades later, these trends have only continued. A study of ten thousand American adults found a 13 percent rise in loneliness between 2018 and 2019.[4] In total, about 60 percent of respondents reported being lonely—and this was before the COVID-19 pandemic. Loneliness was higher among Gen Z respondents, heavy social media users, and those without healthy work-life balance. Another 2018 study, this one by the Pew Research Center, found that 35 percent of American adults have a low level of trust in others; 41 percent had a medium level of trust, and only 22 percent were considered high trusters. The proportion of low trusters was highest among communities of color, Gen Z, and millennials.[5]

Without social connections, individuals suffer. But our societies suffer as well. If you don't feel connected to the people around you, you are far less likely to volunteer or vote. You tend not to follow news and current events. You don't try as hard to understand social issues.[6] If you don't trust your neighbors, community leaders, or elected officials, you're more prone to apathy and cynicism. What that means is you, and those around you, are short on *social capital.*

There are two major types of social capital: *bonding social capital* and *bridging social capital.* Bonding social capital exists between individuals who share similar backgrounds or values. You are bonded by all that you have in common, producing reliable and comfortable relationships that are likely to be sustained over time. Such relationships are essential and healthy, but they can also be insular and exclusive.[7]

Bridging social capital comes out of relationships that reach outside of typical demographics, characteristics, or social groups. Such relationships, which can be personal or professional, usually take more effort to build and maintain. It can be easier to experience misunderstandings or conflict. But bridging social capital also expands our knowledge and understanding, opens up our networks, and increases our tolerance and acceptance of people who are different from us.[8]

The Mississippi Freedom Summer project of 1964, organized by the Student Nonviolent Coordinating Committee (SNCC) and Congress on Racial Equity (CORE), relied heavily on both kinds of social capital. The collective action sent mostly white college students to the most segregated state in the union to push for civil rights. The organizers and volunteers had two major goals: register African Americans to vote and establish Freedom Schools that taught subjects like math, reading, and African American history and culture.

It was *bonding* social capital that drew volunteers in. Sociologists Doug McAdam and Ronnelle Paulsen found that, controlling for other key demographics such as age, gender, college major, and home region, the strongest factor that determined a college student's participation in the Freedom Summer project was a connection to another volunteer. They were also more likely to volunteer if they received support from key people or networks, including parents, friends, religious groups or figures, and civil rights organizations.[9]

But project organizers also understood that *bridging* social capital had to be built between well-off white college students from the North and impoverished, marginalized Black Mississippians, many of whom had never left their communities, let alone interacted with whites as peers. If the volunteers' invitations to register to vote or join a Freedom School—risky, dangerous propositions for any African American in

Mississippi—were to have any legitimacy, the volunteers would have to build trust and demonstrate their commitment.

From the beginning of the project, the student volunteers, who eventually numbered more than seven hundred, went through several stages of building connections with everyone involved. They underwent intensive training in Ohio before being sent to Mississippi. Once on the ground, they lived with Black host families. They "walked through the back side of town, ate in black homes, introduced themselves to black churches, and sat on porches where no white person had ever sat before," according to historian Bruce Watson.[10] Even when the volunteers began canvassing, their first priority was connecting on a personal level. SNCC program director and Mississippi native Lawrence Guyot told the volunteers that canvassing consisted of "surviving and walking around talking to people about what they're interested in." Guyot explained, "Let's say you're riding past a picnic and people are cuttin' watermelons. You don't immediately go and say, 'Stop the watermelon cuttin' and let's talk about voter registrations.' You cut some watermelons."[11] Guyot and his colleagues understood that their civil rights work was only possible if it was built on a foundation of authentic relationships.

In the end, Freedom Summer resulted in the establishment of more than forty Freedom Schools across the state; about 17,000 Black Mississippians attempted to register to vote (though only 1,200 succeeded). The cost was immense: many volunteers, project staff, and Black Mississippians were arrested and beaten. There were bombings and even more bomb threats. Three civil rights activists were murdered. But the international attention the project received, in addition to the public outcry over the horrific treatment of the civil rights activists, paved the way for the Civil Rights Act of 1964 and the Voting Rights Act of 1965.[12]

Clearly, Freedom Summer is the kind of high-risk social justice action that would be unquestionably difficult—and probably traumatizing—for sensitive individuals to participate in. The level of danger, threat, and violence that both Black and white activists were subjected to by white supremacists and Ku Klux Klan members was abhorrent. A number of volunteers went home early. The organizers and volunteers all likely experienced some form of PTSD afterward.[13] It was a bold, risky experiment, executed on a large scale in a volatile time and a relatively lawless geography.

Freedom Summer could not have launched, let alone sustained itself over more than two months in the face of such opposition and violence, without strong ties between everyone involved: the coordinators, the trainers, the bus drivers, the civil rights activists, the students, the host families, and the broader African American community of Mississippi. Through the power of relationships, they were able to recruit a large number of volunteers for an exceptionally dangerous project. They had far greater courage and influence together than alone. They trusted and relied on each other to offer encouragement and to keep one another safe. They redefined how Blacks and whites could collaborate toward a shared goal. And through their collective bonds, they achieved something extraordinary.

The same principles hold true on a micro level—in our everyday lives, with the everyday people we encounter. Remarkable things can happen when we take the time to build relationships with one another, especially those who are different from us. When we spend time with others without an agenda, when we listen for the fuller contexts of childhood and culture, when we tap into new reservoirs of empathy, when we nurture genuine affection for another as *human* before any other label, we have the potential to change—and be changed—on a soul level.

There's even a name for the work of connecting to others for the social good: *relational activism.* According to sociologists Sara O'Shaugnessy and Emily Huddart Kennedy, who coined the term in 2010, "relationship-building work contributes to conventional activism and constitutes activism in and of itself."[14] While far more attention is given to "public-sphere activism," their research of environmental activism found that small, everyday actions done within networks over time provide the background support needed for public actions and contribute to important cultural change.[15] In other words, the very foundation of social movements can be built on the strength of thoughtful, empathic individual interactions.

British NGO professionals Becca Dove and Tim Fisher have found that "person-to-person compassion and the desire to relate can create movement and change where before there was none." Relational activism, they explain, "makes change happen through personal and informal relationships. . . . The aim of the relational activist is to compassionately change the bit of the world we can touch."[16]

Relational activism could come in the form of offering encouragement and inspiration to a person already involved in a cause. It could involve increasing someone else's awareness of or engagement with a social issue. Perhaps you nudge a friend or colleague into volunteering with you. Or maybe you connect with someone who is very different from you—building that bridging social capital—and end up profoundly changing their worldview and expanding their capacity for empathy.

An inspiring example of the power of relational activism can be seen in the work of Daryl Davis. Davis, who is Black, is a musician and actor by profession. His side gig is befriending members of the KKK. He accidentally fell into this when he met a man after a performance in Maryland, who eventually admitted to being a Klan member. Through that first interaction, Davis has connected with a number of other Klan members. He has approached these relationships with curiosity, genuinely wanting answers to a question he has carried since childhood: "Why do you hate me when you know nothing about me?" Through honest conversation and persistent friendship, Davis has so challenged their assumptions that he has been directly responsible for somewhere between forty and sixty individuals leaving the KKK and indirectly responsible for more than two hundred departures.[17]

There is no magic formula to what Davis has done. "One of Davis's methods," explains journalist Nicholas Kristof, "is not to confront antagonists and denounce their bigotry but rather to start in listening mode. Once people feel they are being listened to, he says, it is easier to plant a seed of doubt."[18] Daryl Davis has done what we are all capable of doing to some degree: Be curious. Be respectful. Be understanding. Be kind. Be present. Be yourself. The potential for great change can come from almost any relationship, if we are willing to give it the time, care, and attention it needs to flourish.

I'm guessing most of us don't feel particularly drawn to building friendships with extremists and hate group members. Yet there is probably already someone you know who is different enough that a dialogue and closer connection could be valuable for both of you: someone from a different socioeconomic class, or of a different cultural background, or from another country, or affiliated with another political party, or who sees an issue or cause from a different perspective. Reaching out to those we disagree with or don't understand requires generous listening, humility, patience, hospitality, and "adventurous civility," as the organization Interfaith Philadelphia puts it in their "Better Conversations" guidebook. Adventurous civility is not "a mere matter of politeness or niceness," but instead recognizes "the difficulty of what we face and the complexity of what it means to be human."[19]

The potential impact of extending respect and a listening ear should never be underestimated. According to organizational psychologist Adam Grant, "In over 500 studies, interacting face-to-face with an out-group [i.e., those outside of a particular, clearly defined group] reduced prejudice 94 percent of the time."[20] Grant is not talking about conducting diversity and inclusion trainings, or engaging in debates, or bombarding one another with links to articles that support our view. He is referring to one of the most basic human activities: a civil, respectful face-to-face conversation with another human being. But that simple act is enough to reduce prejudice *almost all the time*. What other social justice activities have that kind of success rate at instigating change?

Probably because it's so simple and within almost anyone's capacity to practice, relational activism also has a wonderful multiplicative effect. Studies have found that those on the receiving end of relational activism have a high likelihood of paying it forward by practicing it themselves, thus widening the circle of civility, conversation, and care. Those who have experienced such healthy, meaningful dialogues report being able to have similar types of conversations with more people about a greater number of sensitive topics.[21]

Our civic life today is defined by divisions and silos, by mistrust and lack of engagement. What would it look like if the highly sensitive and empathic among us decided to flip the script? Many of us already have the natural ability to connect and empathize with people. We tend to listen well and ask thoughtful questions. We enjoy thinking deeply about people and meaningful issues. Perhaps you feel inspired by the chance to direct that energy in a more intentional way, creating space for respectful conversations in hopes of building long-term friendships. It doesn't need to be done efficiently or on a large scale. You could do it where you already are—in your schools, workplaces, families, neighborhoods, and community groups—in the bits of extra time and margin you have available. If you feel drawn to the idea of relational activism, just remember that your simple willingness to listen and share, to build social capital with just a few people around you, could multiply into a tidal wave of trust and goodwill. And trust and goodwill are among the most important currencies of widespread societal change.

A number of organizations across the globe are already promoting such dialogues. Some, like Interfaith Philadelphia and Camden Council, provide training or facilitated discussions that teach skills, provide guidance, and ensure a safe place to put this into practice. Others, such as the Human Library or the Empathy Museum, give you the chance to hear someone else's story.[22] One of the Empathy Museum's exhibits, called "A Mile in My Shoes," encourages visitors to actually put on the shoes of someone from an entirely different lived reality—a refugee, a sex worker, a war veteran—and listen to audio recordings of their stories.[23] As we have seen throughout human history, the story of one person's life—your own and that of others—carries within it the potential to change lives.

Relational activism *is* social activism. And it's the kind of activism that sensitive, empathic people have the potential to excel at. Healthy dialogue leads to healthy relationships, which promote healthy communities and societies. The trends of *Bowling Alone* certainly don't have to continue. Sensitive change agents can show the rest of society what it looks like to connect with one another, face-to-face, as fellow human beings, to be *for* one another even when we are very different from one another. As the relational activists among us engage and learn and care, they can help us create communities that are far more willing to move boulders, climb mountains, and bridge chasms to ensure dignity and equality for all of us.

13

Creatives

"The function of art is to do more than tell it like it is—it's to imagine what is possible."

bell hooks

In 1965, as the United Farm Workers (UFW) began striking for better working conditions in Central California, a young man named Luis Valdez had an idea. Valdez had worked in the fields with his family as a boy and recently joined the picket lines. The recent college graduate had previously performed with the San Francisco Mime Troupe, and decided to approach UFW leader Cesar Chavez to suggest a new initiative.

"One day he said something about a theater, how important it was, and asked if I thought it could be done," Chavez recalled in an oral history recorded in *Cesar Chavez: Autobiography of La Causa*. "I said, 'Yeah, let's try it.'"[1]

With that informal go-ahead, Valdez, along with musician Agustín Lira, recruited a few farmworkers to help them. The group performed a short *acto* for UFW members at a regular

Friday night meeting soon after. There was no script or scenery; the only costumes were signs that the actors wore to identify their characters. The performers, playing multiple roles each, acted out material they had written on their own.[2]

The performance was a hit. The union members, just at the beginning of the bitterly fought Delano Grape Strike and Boycott, loved the creative, humorous, and on-point portrayal of their experiences. Many of the farmworkers could not read or write, but they could see themselves in the performances and improvisations. They clamored for more.

Thus was born El Teatro Campesino (The Farmworkers' Theatre), which became the cultural arm of the UFW and the broader Chicano movement. Its performances were first staged in union halls, on top of flatbed trucks, and in front of picket lines to raise the spirits of striking workers. But its reach quickly expanded. El Teatro Campesino began touring around Central California, increasing awareness of the poor working conditions of farmworkers and raising funds to support the movement. The purpose of El Teatro, according to Valdez, "was to examine and redefine the heart of the Chicano people: ritual, music, beauty, and spiritual sensitivity." For him, theater is a vehicle "to affect and modify and change and give direction to society."[3]

The work of Valdez and his company quickly gained recognition, garnering awards and inspiring the launch of other Chicano theater groups. El Teatro eventually split from the UFW to become an independent entity focusing on a broader range of issues, including education, racism, indigenous identities, and the Vietnam War.[4] El Teatro went on to host annual Chicano theater festivals, and "almost singlehandedly fostered a national theatre movement," according to historians.[5] The theater group still exists today, with Luis Valdez still at the helm, providing a powerful and influential voice for Chicano culture.

Art has an immense power to effect change. Through El Teatro, one humble group of performers gave voice to a marginalized community, raised funds for a cause, increased public awareness of injustices in their midst, grew support for a movement, and inspired an entire generation of activist artists.

Art of all forms can help us see ourselves, others, and our societies in different ways. It can compellingly and viscerally communicate the realities of the human experience through mediums that our senses cannot ignore—even when we might want to turn away. Art is our conscience, calling out where we as humans have gone terribly wrong. Art is our imagination, broadening the horizons of what could be.

When we encounter art, we are changed. In a growing field called neuroaesthetics, neuroscientists are discovering just how deeply impacted we are by creative works. Studies have found that, as humans experience art, multiple regions of our brains are activated and higher-than-normal connections between these regions are observed.[6] We sense, we process, we feel, and we make meaning from art. Aesthetic experiences shape our personal identity, sense of purpose, empathy, imagination, creativity, and human connection. The powerful influence of art on our brains explains why music has been found to reduce stress and pain and to help in treating trauma.[7] Or why reading fiction consistently leads to greater empathy, as encountering the thoughts, emotions, and experiences of someone else can shift how we perceive others.[8]

Every social movement has been fueled and amplified by creative people. They have given voice, expression, agency, and empowerment to the marginalized and oppressed. Their works have brought clarity, cohesion, and energy to activists; their messaging has lodged into the public consciousness through music, poetry, film, graffiti, iconography, literature, photography, sculpture, dance, and other forms of art—even handkerchiefs embroidered with personal messages, created by a small group of "craftivists" and hand-delivered to board members of retail giant Marks & Spencer in 2015 that successfully convinced them to provide living wages for the company's workers.[9]

As sociologist Ron Eyerman explains in his essay, "The Art of Social Movement," "Art practices form the core of the symbolic and expressive aspects of social movements. When created within movement contexts, art reveals truth as the movement sees it. At the same time and through the same process, artistic representations and expressions make the movement visible to itself. . . . The art created within a social movement objectifies the ideas and emotions which motivate and guide that movement, providing a mirror for the movement to know itself. The same processes of objectification and representation make it possible to transmit protest traditions over time and space."[10]

In other words, art helps shape social movements in real time by reflecting back to activists their identity, goals, and strategies. But art also creates a lasting record of activism that influences the generations that follow.

In his book *A People's Art History of the United States: 250 Years of Activist Art and Artists Working in Social Justice Movements*, author and artist Nicolas Lampert traces the role of art in justice in North America as far back as the 1600s. Native American tribes used wampum belts, made from beads and shells strung together, to communicate, negotiate, build alliances, and make agreements with new arrivals from Europe. Those agreements were, as we know, entirely disregarded, but the wampum belts remained as a reminder of the broken promises and what had been stolen from Native communities.[11]

About a century later, the abolitionist movement on both sides of the Atlantic gained significant momentum when a young British clergyman named Thomas Clarkson commissioned architectural drawings of the slave ship *Brookes*, complete with graphic depictions of the cramped and inhumane conditions in which captured Africans were transported. The images, printed and disseminated by the thousands in the United Kingdom, the United States, and major European cities in 1787–89, were so striking that they triggered outrage and led to increased opposition to slavery. The United Kingdom passed its first law against the slave trade in 1792, just a few years later, due in large part to the awareness, knowledge, and empathy fomented and amplified by Clarkson's drawings.[12]

This dynamic collaboration between art and social justice continues today. When actor and singer Harry Belafonte first attended an acting program founded by a Holocaust survivor, the teachers and speakers were very clear that their calling was not performance but social progress. Musician, actor, and activist Paul Robeson told them that "we are the gatekeepers of truth. We not only show life as it is, but our responsibility is to show life as it should be." Others taught that "art is the moral compass of civilization" and "we're the 'radical voice of humanity.'"[13]

Creative works are the heartbeat of social justice movements, fueling activists with perspective, inspiration, and ideas. Creativity is also one of the most recognizable traits of sensitive individuals, who embody a rich and complex tapestry of emotion, sensory awareness, and artistic expression. Elaine Aron has found that "almost all HSPs have an artistic side they enjoy expressing. Or they deeply appreciate some form of art."[14] As writer Pearl S. Buck said, "The truly creative mind in any field is no more than this: A human creature born abnormally, inhumanly sensitive."[15] The sensitive, empathic mind can notice what others don't, can bring together ideas that others wouldn't, can form beauty that others couldn't imagine.

Creativity can be expressed in many forms. Creativity in strategy, organization, planning, communication, marketing, relationship-building, training, and more are all valuable skills that can be applied in almost any industry. But the creative that produces works of art plays a particular role in social justice movements. "When social movements embrace artists," writes Nicolas Lampert, "they harness the power of those who excel at expressing new ideas and reaching people in ways that words and other forms of media cannot. . . . And when artists join movements, their work—and by extension their lives—takes on a far greater meaning. They become agitators in the best sense of the word and their art becomes less about the individual and more about the common vision and aspirations of many. Their art becomes part of a culture of resistance."[16]

When they engage in social activism, artists take part in something bigger and more meaningful outside of themselves. But the creative process also provides real benefits to artists themselves. Making art has been found to be cathartic, healing, and pleasurable, triggering the release of dopamine, serotonin, and oxytocin in our brains that trigger positive emotions.[17] The very process of creating can make us healthier, happier, and more grounded individuals.

But being a creative also comes with real fears and anxieties. Sharing our deeply personal expressions with the wider world can be terrifying, especially for the highly sensitive. The subjective nature of artistic interpretation means that there will always be some who like your work, others who feel apathetic toward it, and others who despise it. It is an inevitable part of the artist's journey to learn to tolerate criticism, negativity, and rejection. And that can be incredibly difficult, even though art can only be part of a culture of resistance if it is shared.

To be a creative in social justice is to exist in a state of paradox: Your art can bring you both deep joy and terrible grief. Your sensitivity both inspires your art and makes it harder to share. Your creative contributions can give you a meaningful role within social movements but also make you a target of naysayers and opponents.

Arguments for the censorship of art and artists date back to at least the fourth century BCE, when Greek philosopher Plato advocated for the sanitization of paintings, music, plays, and poetry. He saw art as merely an imitation of reality, and the messages communicated by art as detrimental to the moral ideal that he and his followers espoused. Plato even went so far as to suggest the expulsion of artists from the city-state of Athens to curtail their influence on fellow citizens.[18]

The persecution of activist artists continues today throughout the world. Chinese artist Ai Weiwei has been exiled from his home country since 2015 for his critiques of the Chinese government's totalitarian control, human rights abuses, and corruption.[19] Iranian filmmaker and musician Hossein Rajabian, his brother Mehdi, and another partner were arrested by security forces and convicted in 2015 of "spreading propaganda against the system" and "insulting the sacred." Among their "crimes" was running a music distribution service without government approval and working with female singers.[20] Burmese poet U Saw Wai was charged in October 2019 for reciting a poem critical of the military control over the government; similarly, Indian poet Siraj Bisarelli was arrested in February 2020 after he publicly read a poem that critiqued a new federal law.[21]

The "State of Artistic Freedom" report of 2020, released by the human rights organization Freemuse, documented 978 acts of violation of artistic freedom in 89 countries and online, a 37 percent increase over 2019. Europe had the highest proportion of incidents, at 26 percent, followed by North and South America at 19 percent. Forty-two artists involved in Black Lives Matters protests were the victims of racially charged violence, and at least twenty-six works of art that served as tributes to George Floyd were vandalized.[22]

These stories and statistics are extremely sobering. But they also speak to the consequential role of creatives in raising awareness, rousing compassion, and rallying people to a cause. Artists are perceived as threats because they are so effective at advocating for change.

To sustain their artistic activism, creatives need community. It's no coincidence that artists tend to cluster together in neighborhoods, workspaces, collectives, and online communities. We need friends, collaborators, peers, and trusted partners to inspire, interpret, and give feedback throughout the creative process. We need supportive people in our lives who will encourage us when our art is criticized or attacked, and inspire us to continue to share our work with the world.

If the arena of activist art sounds too intimidating, that's okay. Artists certainly don't *have* to engage in justice in a confrontational way. Sarah Corbett, founder of the Craftivist Collective that influenced the Marks & Spencer board, calls her approach "slow and mindful activism." "My approach is not aggressive, loud or transactional, but focuses on a gentle art of protesting, threading humility through all that we create and do," she writes.[23] She and her colleagues have directed their efforts toward beauty, kindness, humanity, and love. It is entirely possible that the quiet, gentle work of a single artist can ring as loudly as a protest of thousands.

The last few years have seen several prominent art installations at the US-Mexico border wall championed by Donald Trump. French street artist JR created *Kikito*, a seventy-foot-tall rendition of a Mexican child peering over the border wall into the United States, as well as a long picnic table that extended into both countries and invited Americans and Mexicans to share a meal.[24] California-based architects Ronald Rael and Virginia San Fratello developed *Teeter Totter Wall*, three pink seesaws attached at the wall that invited individuals on both sides of the border to play with one another.[25] These artists have taken a symbol of xenophobia, racial bias, family separation, division, and conflict, and remolded it into a place of play, conversation, community, and profound reflection. They not only changed the physical landscape of the border wall, but they also altered the narrative on immigration and US-Mexico relations by forcing us to recognize our shared humanity.

The most urgent justice matters of our day—income inequality, racial injustice, gender inequality, refugee resettlement, environmental injustice, ethnic conflict, and more—desperately need creative, compassionate, and empathic individuals who can translate the complex and controversial into a medium that transfixes our senses and creates a tangible sense of connection. Activist artists can transform the conversation about an issue, no matter how deeply entrenched and long-standing a challenge may be. Sometimes, they may be the only ones who can.

The activism of the creative soul speaks to all of us. Whether it challenges or comforts, provokes or heals, art forces us to see, think, and act differently. Social change is not possible unless we embrace and empower the artists within us and around us. Creatives show the world what's possible, and inspire us to make that possibility into reality.

14

Record Keepers

"I know of no way of judging the
future but by the past."

Patrick Henry

At the last stop of the Underground Railroad, which led as many as 100,000 enslaved Blacks to freedom in the North, was a man in an office. Those who were fortunate enough to reach this point in the free state of Pennsylvania, led there by heroic crusaders like Harriet Tubman, had battled the wilderness and natural elements. They had evaded security officers and hidden from guard dogs and vigilantes. They were more than ready to experience their first breath of freedom, and William Still was the person who provided the administrative paperwork for that to happen.

Both of Still's parents were former slaves who had managed to secure their freedom before he was born. He taught himself to read and write, skills that became invaluable as he joined the abolitionist movement.[1] By his early twenties, he was working as a clerk for the Pennsylvania Society for the Abolition of Slavery.[2]

While Still supported the cause of antislavery in many ways, including through philanthropy and overseeing a network of safe houses, his most historically significant contribution may have been the records he kept as a conductor on the Underground Railroad. One of those journals still survives today, stored in a vault at the Historical Society of Pennsylvania.

At the top of nearly every page, Still wrote a single word: "Arrived." In neat, flowing cursive, he recorded the names, descriptions, and stories of the escaped slaves he met—what they looked like, where they were from, why they escaped, and who their family members were as well as their new identities and where they were headed next to start a new life.[3]

Some of his fellow abolitionists begged him not to keep such meticulous records. In the wrong hands, the information could be a death sentence for the escaped slaves. But Still persevered in filling journal after journal with the information he cataloged—while also ensuring that they were carefully hidden. Such records were the only hope that formerly enslaved families had of being reunited. And he wanted the world to know the names and experiences of the individuals who had suffered so gravely at the hands of slave owners and the institutions that empowered them. "The heroism and desperate struggle that many of our people had to endure should be kept green in the memory of this and coming generations," he vowed.[4]

His efforts led to the reunification of many formerly enslaved families—including his own reunion with a long-lost brother—but also the publication of the only contemporaneous account of the Underground Railroad in an 1872 book called *The Underground Railroad Chronicles*.[5]

Record makers and record keepers like Still preserve essential information for communities and societies. To be a record *maker* is to capture the detailed conditions of people's lives at a particular moment in time. Their work is a reflection of reality as we understand it to be, providing clear evidence of where we as a society are doing well and where we are not, whom we have shown preference to and whom we have marginalized. It documents how our governments have functioned, the consequences of the decisions our leaders have made, the effectiveness of our institutions, and the inclusiveness of our societies. And record *keeping* ensures that this information is preserved, organized, and made easily accessible to the public.

Today, record makers and record keepers inhabit a broad range of sectors and professions. They may come in the form of secretaries, clerks, historians, archivists, librarians, administrative assistants, stenographers, surveyors, data entry specialists, accountants, videographers, museum curators, information managers, data managers, documentarians, report writers, database administrators, and more. Their skill sets and interests are just as diverse, encompassing activities like developing surveys, interviewing, investigating, writing, typing, recording, filing, collecting, organizing, cataloging, scanning, digitizing, storing, editing, analyzing, presenting, answering questions, and responding to requests.

Upon closer inspection of one particular type of record keeper, an archivist, we see responsibilities that are far-ranging and of critical importance. Archivist and social activist Randall C. Jimerson, whose career was partly inspired by the Watergate investigations and hearings, explains that his work includes "determining what documentary materials will be chosen and protected in the archives; evaluating or appraising the significance of these archival sources; ensuring their preservation from decay, neglect, media instability, and theft; organizing and describing the materials in order to make them accessible for future use; providing access to and reference assistance; promoting knowledge of archival holdings through outreach and public programs; and conducting advocacy on behalf of archives and archival interests."[6] By any measure, this is an impressive job description.

Such individuals are the holders of our collective memory and history, the preservers of vast amounts of wisdom and knowledge about humanity. In all the numbers, charts, lists, and reports are stories of individuals, groups, and entire societies. "I have come to believe that archivists can contribute to a richer human experience of understanding and compassion," explains Jimerson. "Archivists provide resources for people to examine the past, to understand themselves in relation to others, and to deepen their appreciation of people with different backgrounds and perspectives."[7]

Archivists and their fellow record keepers play a critical role in the social justice sphere. According to information scholars Renée Saucier and David A. Wallace, record making, record keeping, and archiving "are vital active sites of social justice and injustice." Authoritative records effectively reflect our contexts, shape our understanding of the past, and provide valuable information for justice movements.[8] They contribute to our ability to understand facts, track and compare data, and hold leaders and institutions accountable—both in the present day and for the historical record. Even in the gaps and silences of our documents, in the information that has been suppressed or was never recorded, we can determine biases, prejudices, and blind spots.[9] We can see whom we have ignored or forgotten or deemed unimportant.

In this current moment in history, the merit of keeping and maintaining records is abundantly clear. Debates about what is fact, what is true, and what is real have become commonplace. "Unfortunately, we live at a moment in which ignorance appears to be one of the defining features of American political and cultural life," cultural studies professor Henry A. Giroux said in a 2016 interview. "Ignorance has become a form of weaponized refusal to acknowledge the violence of the past. . . . The warning signs from history are all too clear. Failure to learn from the past has disastrous political consequences."[10] Without knowledge based on reliable records, our societies cannot understand our past mistakes, how to repair them, or how to prevent them from happening again.

This "organized forgetting," as Giroux calls it, is happening all around the world. A 2018 special report from the Index on Censorship found that authoritarian governments are focusing significant energy on controlling historical narratives—shutting down museums, banning history books, and even imprisoning historians who challenge them.[11]

Such efforts, troubling as they are, are not new. In 1904, for example, a medical doctor and longtime public servant named Peter Bryce began serving as the chief medical officer of the federal Departments of the Interior and Indian Affairs in Canada.[12] One of his high-profile responsibilities was to write and publish an annual report on the health of Indigenous peoples in Canada. He did not hold back. His 1905 and 1906 reports showed that First Nations communities had abnormally high death rates. In 1907, he eviscerated the health conditions in the residential school system, a thinly veiled cultural cleansing and forced assimilation program that Indigenous children between the ages of seven and sixteen were mandated to attend.[13] Bryce reported that Indigenous children did not receive adequate medical attention and lived in unsanitary conditions; he recommended policy changes to improve the health and education services provided. So threatening to the Canadian government was his report that they never released it. Bryce was eventually forced into early retirement in 1921. Nevertheless, his written work stands as a record and testament to the systematic oppression of First Nations peoples and support for the call for reparations. More than a century later, we can still look back and unpack the details of these past injustices, equipping us to prevent and recognize other injustices moving forward.

Today, whenever there are large-scale human rights abuses, one of the first steps aid workers and activists take is to document the names and stories of victims and survivors, much like William Still did. This allows them to build a case, proving (1) that such atrocities happened or are happening, (2) the scale of and systems behind the atrocities, and (3) which perpetrators are responsible for the human rights violations. The gathering of details reveals the identities of those affected and tracks any documentation they may have shared (identification documents, land titles, citizenship records, employment records, etc.), which in turn determines which rights have been violated and lays the groundwork for possible future reparations.[14]

Before founding the human rights NGO International Justice Mission, lawyer Gary Haugen served as director of the UN investigation into the 1994 genocide of ethnic Tutsis and moderate Hutus in Rwanda. Much of Haugen's work involved visiting massacre sites and mass graves. He recorded the stories of those who had been killed through the personal belongings and identification papers they clutched in death as well as the testimonies of survivors. "These mass graves might appear as vague, dark images of generalized evil in an unjust world," he reflected years later, "but in truth they were an intimate family portrait with a story for every face—each member of the human family having lived and died as one individual at a time."[15] The efforts of Haugen and others like him restore humanity, dignity, and value to fellow human beings who have suffered greatly. And their information-gathering enables justice. After the Rwandan genocide, for the first time in history, an international criminal tribunal was able to convict dozens of leaders—military officials, government officials, leaders of religion and media, and more—of committing genocide.[16]

Knowledge of the past, if fully brought to light, is an incredibly empowering tool of the people. Governments the world over recognize the essential role record keeping plays in promoting accountability, countering corruption, and protecting human rights in the public sphere.[17] As a result, authority figures often try to control records and the people who create them. Dedicated, conscientious record makers and record keepers who care deeply about truth and representation of the marginalized serve as vital ballasts in the halls of power, contributing "to the embedding of a new human rights culture," according to researchers in the *Journal of Human Rights Practice*.[18]

So crucial is this work that the United Nations High Commissioner for Human Rights has explicitly asserted that states have the responsibility to ensure that archives of any human rights abuses are preserved and accessible.[19] And the Human Rights Working Group of the International Council on Archives declared that such archives are foundational to the "adequate protection of the human rights and fundamental freedom to which all persons are entitled, be they economic, social and cultural, or civil and political."[20]

In a hopeful trend, record making has become increasingly democratized. Nowadays nearly anyone with an interest in documenting injustice has the tools to do so—through smart phones, tablets, written records, and other mediums. How many incidents of injustice have you learned about because of a video recorded by a bystander? Black Lives Matter and global protests against police brutality have been fueled by eyewitness videos of the unjust killings of Eric Garner, Philando Castile, and George Floyd, among far too many others. The "citizen journalists" who recorded these videos altered cultural narratives by providing irrefutable evidence and propelling social movements forward. Our communities benefit greatly from dedicated professional documentarians *and* ordinary citizens who step into the role when needed.

In many ways, sensitive individuals are ideal record makers and keepers. Our empathy, attention to detail, and intuitive sense of what's missing allow us to approach this work with care and conscientiousness. But being such a witness to history is not without risk to our tender hearts and souls.

Consider those who serve as frontline documentarians of injustice. Such work can involve conducting interviews or completing surveys with survivors of trauma. Empathy is an invaluable skill for interviewers in such cases. Studies have shown that those who interview survivors of trauma or others in duress are far more effective when they can practice empathetic communication. Whether in medicine, social work, or investigative journalism, interviewers tend to collect more accurate information, thoughts, and feelings from interview subjects when they express kindness, patience, and understanding.[21]

At the same time, hearing stories of suffering can easily cause secondary trauma. Even one instance of record making can lead to emotional scarring. Darnella Frazier was only seventeen years old when she recorded the ten-minute video of George Floyd's murder at the hands of Minneapolis police officers. A year later, she explained, "I still hold the weight and trauma of what I witnessed a year ago. It's a little easier now, but I'm not who I used to be. A part of my childhood was taken from me."[22]

We risk exhausting our emotional reserves when we place ourselves in situations where we are regularly absorbing the pain, grief, and anger of others. Perhaps your heart can handle this. As important as this work is, I know my soul and those of many others who are sensitive could not bear it. Fortunately, there are plenty of other activities in the realm of record keeping that are just as important but allow for more emotional distance. Many of these have to do with analyzing, preserving, organizing, and sharing information. Any number of sectors and social issues benefit from careful record keeping, including but certainly not limited to environmental justice, public health, redlining, financial inclusion, disability rights, education, and human trafficking.

And with the expansion of new technologies, individuals with strong technical skills also play an important role in gathering and maintaining records. When the COVID-19 pandemic first reached the United States in early 2020, for example, it was accompanied by a spike in anti-Asian rhetoric and hate crimes. A group of activists created a multilingual website called Stop AAPI Hate, inviting any Asian or Asian American individual who had experienced some form of hate to submit their stories. I went to the site to add to the growing number of records after a stranger yelled racial epithets at my children and me, telling us to "go home." While an exceedingly painful experience for me, the ability to immediately record what had happened in a user-friendly online interface, and the knowledge that it would not be forgotten, brought some comfort. In large part due to the real-time record keeping work of Stop AAPI Hate, the surge of anti-Asian hate received national attention, rallying agencies and community groups to respond.[23]

We no longer need to rely on someone like William Still to handwrite each individual story we encounter. But in the face of organized forgetting, we still desperately need documentarians of all kinds of skills and abilities. "When we lack historical understanding, we lose part of our identity," writes racial justice advocate Latasha Morrison. "We don't know where we came from and we don't know what there is to celebrate or lament."[24] The stories of all of humanity, but especially those of the marginalized and oppressed, owe their ongoing existence to the record makers and keepers among us. Only when we have a clear sense of where we've been can we begin to chart a way forward.

15
Builders

"Science can amuse and fascinate us all, but
it is engineering that changes the world."
Isaac Asimov

Johannes Gutenberg, as far as we know, was not interested in revolution. The German inventor and goldsmith was primarily interested in making money when he perfected his Gutenberg press in 1450.

While humans have been in the printing business for centuries—the oldest printed material, uncovered by archaeologists in China, dates back to the first millennium CE—Gutenberg introduced several key innovations that allowed for mass-quantity printing. He replaced woodblocks with metal, used replica casting to create molds of letters, mixed his own ink that adhered particularly well to metal, and flattened printing paper with a winepress.[1] The resulting machine could print materials much faster and at a far lower cost than any of its predecessors.[2] Even then, it took him three years to print two hundred copies of the Latin-language Bible we call the Gutenberg Bible—an extraordinary speed compared to the fifteen months it previously took for a scribe to copy a single Bible by hand.[3]

It took many more years to establish a multinational distribution network for books and news, and to see an increase in literacy rates to enable sufficient demand for printed works—by which time Gutenberg had died poor and relatively obscure, his beloved presses repossessed by financiers before his death.

But his technology, according to Francis Bacon, father of the scientific method, changed "the appearance and state of the whole world."[4] What Gutenberg had hoped would be a ticket to personal success instead became a vehicle for social revolution. The printing press not only enabled the mass production of printed material, from news sheets to Martin Luther's "95 Theses," but also ensured the accurate replication of news, literature, and information. No matter someone's income or social status, it was possible for them to access the same pool of knowledge as the wealthiest, most educated elites.

What followed was an explosion in literacy rates, which has doubled every century since the press's first printings. Libraries were established for the first time. Journalism blossomed. Schools were transformed. Communities came together to read, debate, and discuss. Scientists, novelists, historians, philosophers, poets, and inventors could share their groundbreaking work with colleagues and the general public, fueling the Renaissance and the Scientific Revolution.[5] As the printed word spread around the globe, the chains of power that a select few held over the masses due to their superior access to information and knowledge were broken.

Today, many of our societies are awash in technology. In affluent countries, we have come to be wary of the many devices that fill our homes, workplaces, schools, cars, and pockets. We bemoan how technology has weakened social connections, shortened attention spans, obliterated work-life balance, stifled creativity, and minimized physical activity.[6] These are all legitimate concerns.

But technology, *Merriam-Webster* tells us, is nothing more than "the practical application of knowledge especially in a particular area."[7] In our alarm over the potential harm caused by the latest creations filling our store shelves and hard drives, we may be losing sight of an important truth: technology remains one of the most powerful tools at our disposal when it comes to bettering the human condition.

A single invention like the printing press or the light bulb can bring massive improvements to the quality of life for many. A new device, like the light, agile, and customizable Quickie wheelchair invented by Marilyn Hamilton in the 1980s, can empower an entire group of people.[8] Today, novel technologies can still open up new realms of learning, opportunity, and health for large populations.

In the twenty-first century, there are still 840 million people (nearly 11 percent of the global population) who do not have access to electricity. Almost three billion people do not have access to clean cooking.[9] One billion people live more than two kilometers away from an all-weather road.[10] Globally, about 1.7 billion adults are unbanked, or do not have access to a bank account or financial institution, including more than 14 million adults in the United States.[11] Two-thirds of school-age children, or 1.3 billion children, do not have an internet connection in their homes.[12]

And while the printing press was an important step in promoting widespread literacy, we are still falling short in this area. More than 250 million children worldwide do not have access to books or education.[13] This includes the United States, where vast "book deserts" exist in neighborhoods of concentrated poverty and hundreds of students may be asked to share a single textbook.[14]

These are massive inequities that cannot be solved by simply throwing money at the problem or sending a bunch of good-hearted people to build power lines and schools. If it were that easy, these challenges would have been addressed long ago. What such issues require is a significant investment in research and innovation. We need passionate, thoughtful inventors, product designers, programmers, and engineers who can take the time to understand the root issues that curtail rights and access, developing innovative technologies that directly address those challenges.

Consider education access for children around the world. At first glance, we might assume that communities simply need more school buildings, teachers, books, and school supplies. A shortage of these resources certainly contributes to the problem. But the reasons children do not attend school are far more varied and complex. In Kenya, for example, more than one million adolescent girls regularly miss school or drop out of school entirely because they lack access to sanitary pads. This is tied to poverty, yes, but also a dearth of health education and affordable supplies.

Megan Mukuria is an American transplant who now lives in Nairobi, Kenya. Megan cofounded the social enterprise ZanaAfrica, which provides comprehensive women's health resources for young women, including a confidential advice line, health lessons for three cents a day, and a free teen magazine.[15] She and her team (comprised almost entirely of Africans from different countries across the continent) also sell their own brand of sanitary pad and underwear designed specifically for the market they serve.

Why did ZanaAfrica have to create their own sanitary pads? The sanitary pads that are typically available in developed countries don't serve the poorest households. They usually come in packs of twenty or more, making them more expensive. They are designed to be changed a few times a day, increasing the overall cost to cover one menstrual cycle. In sub-Saharan Africa, sanitary pads are often the second most expensive item required for raising girls, behind only bread. Many families in

Kenya can't afford this, so they tend to go without—forcing girls to miss school during their monthly cycles.

A product need wasn't being met, and that gap had huge ramifications for female education, reproductive health, and empowerment. So ZanaAfrica designed their own high-quality, low-cost sanitary pads that last an entire day, enabling girls to make it through a whole school day without having to change it. They created packs as small as a four-pack—about enough to cover a single menstrual cycle—that cost only thirty-five cents. And all the packaging, marketing, and branding have been carefully designed by the ZanaAfrica team to proclaim messages about female pride, strength, beauty, and empowerment, in hopes of breaking stigmas about menstruation and reproductive health.

One of the greatest injustices of our era is that the vast majority of products and services on the market are designed for the 10 percent wealthiest consumers.[16] These are, of course, the people who have the most money and are willing to buy things that they may or may not actually need—an attractive customer base for businesses, entrepreneurs, and inventors of all stripes. As a result, we now have hundreds of millions of people overrun with so much technology that it may cause them more harm than good while billions of their fellow humans lack the basic technologies to move out of poverty.

Paul Polak, whose family fled as refugees from Czechoslovakia when he was a young boy, is often acknowledged as the founder of a relatively new field called *design thinking.* In his classic book, *Out of Poverty: What Works When Traditional Approaches Fail*, he wrote, "For the past twenty-five years, two questions have kept my curiosity aroused: What makes poor people poor? And what can they do about their poverty?"[17] His background in psychiatry and his natural curiosity served him well as he visited subsistence farmers around the world to learn—without any prior assumptions—what their lives were like and what could actually improve their well-being.

His organization, International Development Enterprises, has designed practical, low-cost products like bamboo treadle water pumps and drip-irrigation systems that significantly increase farm productivity and enable farmers to increase their income. Other high-profile organizations, like design firm IDEO and the Hasso Plattner Institute of Design at Stanford University, have taken inspiration from Polak and his design principles. Many universities around the world now offer courses or degrees centered on design thinking or user-centered design.

Engineering and *empathy* are two words that we rarely hear together. But this is the genius of design thinking and why it has wonderful potential as a space for sensitive, empathic individuals. "Design thinking *starts with empathy*, a deep human focus, in order to gain insights which may reveal new and unexplored ways of seeing, and courses of action to follow in bringing about preferred situations for business and society," explain product designers Rikke Friis Dam and Teo Yu Siang.[18] Empathy is at the very heart of creating products and technologies that address major social inequities. It is about meeting people where they are, observing, asking questions, listening, understanding, and collaborating—all areas in which sensitive people excel.

Without this deep understanding of marginalized populations and their desires, needs, limitations, resources, environments, social networks, and distribution systems—which are rarely what they're assumed to be—technological solutions are almost certain to fail. Time and time again we've seen well-intentioned aid programs and for-profit efforts miss the mark. A water treatment center outside Hyderabad, India, inadequately served community members because the five-gallon jerrycan they required for water collection was too heavy for customers to carry.[19] A fish processing plant built near Lake Turkana in Kenya was supposed to provide jobs and exports but closed after only a few days because the local Turkana people had no history of fishing or eating fish—and no interest in doing so.[20] Computer kiosks set up in rural areas of Madhya Pradesh, India, were barely operational due to a lack of electricity and internet connectivity.[21] Large-scale mosquito net distributions in sub-Saharan Africa resulted in millions of families using the insecticide-treated nets to fish instead of protecting themselves from malaria because they considered food a far greater priority, resulting in overfishing while adding carcinogens to drinking water.[22]

Even when backed by well-known leaders, multinational organizations, and massive financial resources, engineering without empathy can be wasteful and may lead to severe unintended consequences.

But when product design and engineering are done right, the resulting technology can have a profound impact on millions or even billions of people. For example, mobile money, which allows consumers to easily store and transfer funds through an app on their mobile phones, has exploded in popularity in Africa and Southeast Asia since it was first introduced by mobile network provider Safaricom in 2007. As many as 1.2 billion people today have mobile money accounts, with more than $2 billion being transacted every single day.[23] Mobile money platforms operate like banks for those who don't otherwise have access to financial institutions, giving them a place to safely store funds. They create channels for consumers to pay for goods and services, and merchants to receive payment without credit cards, checkbooks, exact change, or even face-to-face interactions. The platforms have also reduced corruption and theft, as password-protected mobile money is far more difficult to steal than cash.

Another example of effective design thinking is the line of solar-powered lights that d.light, the company my husband cofounded, designs and sells. These products provide far more than renewable energy. Having access to reliable light at night opens the door to many other opportunities, including increased work hours that result in higher incomes; increased study hours that elevate education outcomes for children; better safety for families who can more easily avoid snakes and other dangerous nocturnal animals; and improved health because families no longer need to burn kerosene oil inside their homes.

Technologies that truly empower people and enable social change are not simple to design or build. They must be tailored specifically to the needs of the target population while still being extremely affordable. Many of the products available in affluent countries would not work elsewhere. Money transfer apps in the United States, for example, typically require a smartphone, charge relatively high fees, and come with bells and whistles that users in other countries would find a nuisance. In contrast, mobile money apps in Africa and Asia have been specifically made for their consumers: compatible with the simplest mobile phones, simple and straightforward to use, and able to handle the smallest of financial transactions, all while charging minimal fees.

Similarly, the solar-powered lanterns made by d.light and other companies are far more rugged, reliable, and long-lasting than those you would find in a sporting goods store in North America or Europe. These lights are in use almost twenty-four hours a day (either turned on for use or charging) and able to withstand a range of conditions, from monsoons to being trampled by livestock. And the products must be affordable for families who can't afford to pay more than a few dollars at a time. In the early days of d.light, we used to ring a bell in the office and celebrate each time the design and engineering teams figured out a new way to cut even one cent out of the cost of a product—from shortening a wire (thus requiring fewer raw materials) to switching to a faster-drying glue (speeding up production time). We knew that every cent mattered, allowing more families to access life-changing solar light.

The arena of design thinking, user-centered design, or designing "for the other 90 percent," as Paul Polak used to say, has taken off in recent years. In just the last two decades, we've witnessed remarkable innovations in agriculture, health, energy, and connectivity. Inventors and dreamers, designers and engineers from all around the world have come up with low-cost, high-quality, user-centered technologies as varied as clean cookstoves, baby incubators, laptops, CT scanners, televisions, vitamins, water filters, and mosquito repellents. But there is still so much more to be done.

The call to develop technologies for the most underserved communities in the world needs to be answered by people who are remarkably creative, who care about the details, are thorough in thinking through a problem, and intuitively understand what people need and want. We need visionary, technically savvy individuals who listen well and connect deeply, who can understand potential consumers and have the patience to generate and iterate upon new ideas until they hit on the best possible solution.

Engineering with empathy is both people work and creative work, providing a great balance between relational time and individual time. It is as much about the heart as the head. Much of the effort takes place on drafting tables and computers, in workshops and cubicles and factories—not the places we would normally associate with social progress, but an essential front in the effort to find relevant, practical, and sustainable solutions to incredibly challenging problems.

The field requires deeply empathic, sensitive people who can help build the tools that enable a more equitable future. Their vision and creativity can lead to products, services, apps, and programs that open up new possibilities and expand access to education, income, health, and more. The legacy of the justice-oriented inventors, designers, and engineers among us will be tangible and transformative for billions of our fellow human beings, changing the ways we live and the opportunities open to us—and likely spur additional innovations for generations to come.

16

Equippers

"Education is our passport to the future, for tomorrow belongs to the people who prepare for it today."

Malcolm X

When I was in elementary school, the story of Rosa Parks's refusal to give up her seat on a Montgomery, Alabama, bus was framed to me as a bit of accidental history, as though segregation and oppression happened to collide with Parks when she was having a particularly bad day. After a long workday on December 1, 1955, the story went, the department store seamstress was just too tired to give up her seat in the "colored" section for a white passenger. And by her simple—albeit spontaneous—act of resistance, she ignited the Montgomery Bus Boycott that would forever alter the course of the civil rights movement.

Perhaps this is the version you learned as well. But the reality is that Rosa Parks knew exactly what she was doing; she had been preparing for this moment for years. She had joined the Montgomery chapter of the NAACP back in 1943, serving as the chapter's secretary for nearly fourteen years. In her role, she investigated atrocities against African Americans and organized campaigns. She also volunteered with the League of Women Voters in the 1940s.

But perhaps most significant, in the summer of 1955, only months before her confrontation on the bus, Parks attended the Highlander Folk School, an education center for civil rights activists in Monteagle, Tennessee.[1]

Founded by educators and activists Myles Horton and Don West in 1932, the Highlander Folk School was initially designed to empower Appalachian rural workers suffering from the Great Depression by teaching them leadership, community building, cultural preservation, and union organizing. The school pursued a democratic model of education: students were encouraged to discuss their own community's challenges and collectively come up with possible solutions.[2]

As tensions around race and segregation escalated in the early 1950s, Highlander pivoted to focus on supporting the civil rights movement, welcoming Black activists from across the South to its residential programs and becoming one of the only fully integrated schools in the region. "The school molded activists into leaders. These leaders, in turn, took what they learned at Highlander directly to the people in their communities,"[3] explain authors Sheila Hardy and P. Stephen Hardy.

Highlander taught valuable lessons about leadership, interpersonal relations, race relations, organizing, and nonviolent resistance. For African Americans who wanted to register to vote in the South, the school also provided citizenship courses and literacy lessons led by civil rights leaders like Septima Clark. In addition, Highlander powerfully modeled the values it encouraged, with workshops co-led by Black and white facilitators and fully integrated meal times.

"I found out for the first time in my adult life that this could be a unified society, that there was such a thing as people of differing races and backgrounds meeting together in workshops and living together in peace and harmony," said Rosa Parks of her time there.[4] Four months later, she changed history.

"Educational work during social movement periods provides the best opportunity for multiplying democratic leadership," wrote Myles Horton, sometimes called "the Father of the Civil Rights Movement," years later in his autobiography.[5] The Highlander Folk School influenced not only Parks but also John Lewis, Marion Barry, Ralph Abernathy, Diane Nash, James Bevel, Martin Luther King, and members of the Student Nonviolent Coordinating Committee (SNCC).

So pivotal was the school's role in training leaders for the civil rights movement that it was repeatedly targeted by the media, segregationists, and political leaders. The state of Tennessee eventually forced it to close in 1961, revoking the school's license and confiscating its property. (The next day, the school reopened as the Highlander Research and Education Center in Knoxville. And it continues to operate today in New Market, Tennessee, focusing on organizing and leadership development for Latinx immigrants and young people.)[6]

Sensitive or not, nobody is born knowing how to create social change. It is something we learn—perhaps from history, but more likely from parents, educators, mentors, community leaders, experts, collaborators, and others. Social movements are built on people, and those people require knowledge, training, and practice to be effective. This knowledge then needs to be passed on to other communities and generations because social movements inevitably last beyond any single lifetime. Many movements go on for decades; some may never end at all. We need multiple generations of change agents to generate social progress. Ideally, each successive generation will have the opportunity to learn from the generations before.

The women's suffrage movement in the United States, which lasted more than seventy years before American women were granted the right to vote, provides an excellent picture for how knowledge and expertise can be passed from one generation to another. The movement traces its roots to Lucretia Mott, born into a Quaker family in 1793—only seventeen years after the United States was established. She and her husband, James, were dedicated, outspoken abolitionists. A passionate orator, Mott also began advocating for women's rights and gender equality as a speaker and Quaker minister.

At the age of forty-seven, Mott met Elizabeth Cady Stanton, a well-educated woman from a prominent family who was twenty years her junior. They met at an antislavery convention in London, where they bonded when the male abolitionists outvoted the female abolitionists to keep women out of the convention.[7] According to biographer Lori D. Ginzberg, "In Mott, Stanton discovered her first female role model: a freethinker, an advocate of women's rights, and a patient mentor, who encouraged the younger woman 'to pursue all the enquiries of thy open, generous confiding spirit.'"[8] Eight years later, in 1848, the two friends helped organize the Seneca Falls Convention, which, controversially, added the words *woman* or *women* throughout the Declaration of Independence, alongside eighteen grievances of women that addressed wide-ranging issues including property ownership, divorce, and the right to vote.[9]

Three years later, a younger Susan B. Anthony joined the movement, and she and Stanton became inseparable.[10] Five years Stanton's junior, Anthony "thrived under Stanton's tutelage—soaking up her knowledge of politics, the law, philosophy, and rhetoric," writes scholar Judith E. Harper.[11] Their partnership and advocacy contributed to several major reforms, including the Fourteenth and Fifteenth Amendments, which gave Black men the rights to due process and to vote, as well as state legislation that gave women the right to own property.

When, in 1892, the seventy-two-year-old Susan B. Anthony finally retired as president of the American Women Suffrage Association, she had already invested in the next generation of leadership. "Anthony spent enormous energy cultivating the most capable of its young women leaders. The most promising of these candidates were Carrie Chapman Catt and Anna Howard Shaw, both of whom eventually served as NAWSA presidents," explains Harper. It would be another twenty-eight years, fourteen years after Anthony's death, that the Nineteenth Amendment giving women the right to vote was finally ratified on August 26, 1920.

When Lucretia Mott first began speaking out for women's rights in the early nineteenth century, not a single country in the world allowed women to vote. The progress she and her collaborators were agitating for required such major cultural and political shifts that multiple generations of women had to contribute, inspiring and teaching one another as they attempted dozens of different strategies over time. Their efforts could very well have taken even longer if they did not prioritize the mentorship, training, and leadership development of younger activists.

A similar story could be told about the abolitionist movement, the disability rights movement, the LGBTQ movement, and other movements. "Through mentoring, the human face of history is shared with the next generation, and we see how mentoring relationships sustain the efforts to build and expand civil rights and human rights through working for social change," explain educators Eli A. Wolff and Dr. Mary Hums.[12]

Teaching and mentoring are areas where sensitive, empathic individuals often thrive. In traditional educational settings, teachers who are sensitive tend to be more attuned to the needs of their students and have a better sense of what help they require and when.[13] Their close attention to detail and their preference for planning and organization enable strong curriculum development, lesson planning, and pedagogy. Their inclusiveness and congeniality make it more likely that students receive the attention and guidance they need. In schools all across the world, sensitive teachers are essential frontline advocates in the fight to expand knowledge, opportunities, and access to more individuals, especially those from marginalized and underserved communities.

Unfortunately, the traditional classroom model can also present real challenges for sensitive teachers, including long hours, extensive interpersonal interactions, and heavy expectations. One survey of over one hundred teachers from high-need schools in urban areas found a strong correlation between sensory processing sensitivity, and emotional exhaustion and burnout.[14]

But as the Highland Folk School and the women's suffrage movement demonstrate, teaching, training, and mentoring in support of social justice can come in many different forms. The traditional classroom model is only one option. Other possibilities for equipping activists include investing in one-on-one relationships, teaching in small groups, facilitating trainings, writing curriculums, giving talks, recording podcasts, designing presentations, hosting retreats, offering consulting services, or creating websites.

My own work in social justice has been deeply informed by classes, books, publications, a training and internship program, informational interviews, sermons, lectures, articles, webinars, conferences, and ad hoc workshops. Each of these resources was provided by someone with expertise, whether a professor, facilitator, practitioner, manager, consultant, spiritual leader, writer, journalist, researcher, or speaker. Some have been tailored for people working or volunteering for a cause. Others have been relevant for a broader audience, such as bystander intervention trainings that provide anyone with practical tools for interrupting race-, gender-, or sexual orientation-based harassment. Other programs empower marginalized or under-represented groups with knowledge and skills.

Teaching, advising, coaching, and mentoring can be highly flexible activities—a major plus for sensitive souls with finite time and energy. It can be done formally or informally, as part of an organization or in your free time. It can be paid or unpaid. It can be a significant item in your schedule or something you do only when you have extra margin to offer. It can be directed toward an experienced social justice professional, someone who is only beginning to wonder about questions of equality and human dignity, or someone who hasn't had access to quality education and training. Learning can happen within businesses and nonprofits, religious institutions and government agencies, or social groups and online networks.

If you choose to provide expertise and guidance to fellow activists, your contributions can help make their engagement more sustainable—no matter how long they have been in the arena. The number one reason people stay in a job, according to a LinkedIn study, is when their organization invests in helping them learn.[15]

Each of us needs to receive knowledge and encouragement as much as we give away our time and energy. And as we share priceless wisdom and inspiration with one another, we can foster a culture of abundance and generosity among activists that counters the culture of expected self-sacrifice and self-martyrdom. We can help build social justice-oriented groups or organizations that are actively promoting learning, training, coaching, and mentorship while authentically valuing the activists themselves.

That doesn't, of course, mean that all teaching is good teaching. Decades of diversity, equity, and inclusion (DEI) trainings in corporations and other large institutions have sometimes netted unintended consequences and surprisingly poor results. The goals of DEI trainings are certainly admirable: equip your people to be more culturally sensitive and culturally competent; reveal prejudices and biases that put certain demographics at a disadvantage; and, ultimately, cultivate more equitable and diverse organizations and communities.

But an extensive study of more than eight hundred companies, conducted by researchers at Harvard University and Tel Aviv University, found that diversity and attitudes toward minority groups *worsened* at organizations five years after they mandated diversity training for employees.[16] As might be expected, people don't tend to respond well to being forced to learn something they don't think they need to learn. And the recent trend of focusing on topics like white privilege and white fragility, often taught in a top-down, lecture-style format, has also backfired. It turns out very few of us, no matter who we are, take kindly to being told by an authority figure or stranger that we are prejudiced or unfairly privileged, or that who we are is fundamentally wrong. One common response from participants in DEI trainings was that they felt targeted, defensive, and hemmed in—possibly causing them to act out in worse ways than before.[17] "A lot of our research shows training makes the dominant group—usually white men—feel threatened and fearful of being excluded," explains researcher Alexandra Kalev. "They fight back instead of internalizing."[18]

To simply tell people why they're wrong and what they need to change doesn't work. It is teaching, mentorship, and coaching—processes that encourage empathy, genuine connection, and flourishing—that help generate change. "Teacher empathy," according to an article in the journal *College Teaching*, "is the degree to which an instructor works to deeply understand students' personal and social situations, to feel care and concern in response to students' positive and negative emotions, and to respond compassionately without losing the focus on student learning."[19] This holds true even when the student has a very different background and may understand the world in starkly different ways.

"All individuals are complex and multifaceted," explains writer and Theory of Enchantment founder Chloé Valdary, who pursues a more empathic approach to DEI trainings. "If we treat any human being, any group of people, as a conglomerate, we run the risk of stereotyping them, reducing them, in our words and in our actions, and turning them into an abstraction. That's not going to be helpful or sustainable for anyone. We have to treat each other like family."[20]

In the area of teaching and mentorship, the empathy that sensitives naturally carry is an invaluable gift that can reach more people and take them further in their learning. We can build up others by authentically living out the values we teach, relying on the best pedagogy available, and genuinely caring for the well-being of those we're guiding. Our best efforts fizzle if we fail to see those we are trying to reach as our peers and allies, our neighbors and friends, or if we fail to deeply respect who they are and who they are trying to become.

When training programs and mentorship or coaching relationships are done well, however, the result could be a new generation of well-informed, well-equipped advocates for social progress. When sensitive people pass along invaluable knowledge, best practices, research, strategies, ideas, and more, we support others in contributing to the causes we dearly love. By doing so, we give them a better chance of creating change, of nudging all of us toward better, fairer societies. We can equip the next generation of informed, engaged, motivated change makers who, like Rosa Parks, are ready to alter history.

17

Researchers

"A little Learning is a dangerous Thing."

Alexander Pope

Embedded in the fourteen-page unanimous decision of the US Supreme Court case *Brown v. Board of Education of Topeka*, penned by Chief Justice Earl Warren, is this passage: "To separate [Black children] from others of similar age and qualifications solely because of their race generates a feeling of inferiority as to their status in the community that may affect their hearts and minds in a way unlikely ever to be undone."[1]

The 1954 landmark ruling, which overturned the separate-but-equal doctrine established in *Plessy v. Ferguson* and paved the way for the end of legal segregation across the United States, was the culmination of five separate class-action lawsuits and years of legal efforts by the NAACP. It also highlighted the efforts of dozens of social scientists, who had been quietly laboring long before *Brown* to document the devastating effects of racism and Jim Crow laws on African Americans.

Two of those researchers were husband-wife psychologists Kenneth Clark and Mamie Phipps Clark. They were the first and second African Americans, respectively, to graduate from Columbia University with doctorates in psychology. In the 1930s, the Drs. Clark had conducted an experiment in Harlem with Black children aged three to seven, using four dolls that were identical except for one thing: two of the dolls had white skin; two had brown skin. (The Clarks had to paint the brown dolls themselves, as no nonwhite dolls were sold at the time.) The researchers asked the children several simple questions, inquiring which dolls were "nice," which were "bad," which they wanted to play with, and which were most like them. That last question in particular incited strong responses from the children. A number of them refused to answer; others would burst into tears and run out of the room. A majority of the Black children—almost all of whom attended segregated schools—showed a consistent preference for the white dolls and considered the brown dolls "bad" and inferior.[2]

In an interview for the civil rights documentary *Eyes on the Prize*, Kenneth Clark explained, "The Dolls Test was an attempt on the part of my wife and me to study the development of the sense of self-esteem in children." They worked with Black children "to see the extent to which their color, their sense of their own race, and status, influenced their judgment about themselves, self-esteem."[3] After being approached by NAACP lead prosecutor Thurgood Marshall about the *Brown* case, the Clarks replicated their experiment once again in 1950, but this time in Southern communities. The findings were the same.

Dr. Kenneth Clark testified in several of the lower court cases that led to *Brown*; he authored a summary of all the scientific findings that supported the plaintiffs' cases, endorsed by thirty-five leading social scientists, that was provided to the Supreme Court.[4] "My opinion is that a fundamental effect of segregation is basic confusion in the individuals and their concepts about themselves conflicting in their self images," he testified in one of the earlier cases. This damage to self-image and self-esteem, this sense that people of darker skin tones were inferior, was taking shape in children even before they could articulate what race was—and would likely remain with them for a lifetime.[5]

The primary findings of the Doll Test were implied in Justice Warren's opinion when he wrote how segregation in schools led Black children to develop "a feeling of inferiority . . . in a way unlikely ever to be undone." With the rigorous research conducted by the Clarks and other dedicated scientists, the arguments against segregation could be backed by scientific evidence that had been replicated again and again over nearly two decades before *Brown* went to trial. The Clarks and others had proven the harmful effects of racism, prejudice, and segregation, which contributed to the justices' ruling that "separate but equal" was anything but.

This is the power of researchers among us. They dig into issues. They ask questions. They challenge assumptions. They study. They theorize. They experiment. They prove and disprove. They establish detailed pictures of human bodies, minds, relationships, communities, the human condition, and the environment around us. They empower societies to make wise, fair, compassionate, and just decisions.

To be represented in scientific study is to be seen, to be counted, to be acknowledged as important. A significant number of systemic inequities are the result of untested theories and incomplete or faulty studies, especially in fields like biology, public health, psychology, sociology, economics, and political science. Without appropriate data, false assumptions about certain categories or groups of people are allowed to perpetuate. Laws and policies are then created based on conclusions drawn from false or limited study. Essential products and services are tailored for the needs of one particular demographic (usually adult, white, cisgender males) without consideration for the differing needs of others. Imaginary problems receive disproportionate public attention while real challenges are overlooked altogether. Public debate on important topics isn't substantive or factually based.

In the field of psychology, for example, the historical reality is that "members of underrepresented groups have been excluded from psychological research . . . stereotyped . . . and in some instances abused."[6] One such failure was the 1952 classification of homosexuality as a "sociopathic personality disturbance" in the American Psychological Association's first *Diagnostic and Statistical Manual of Mental Disorders (DSM-I)*. The classification was founded on shoddy research and guesswork, and it was devastating for the LGBTQ community. Discrimination against gays and lesbians was given pseudoscientific justification. Many underwent cruel psychological and medical treatments as a result. And the voices of LGBTQ individuals were assumed to be unreliable, unreasonable, and unimportant. Researchers, scientists, and academics had made a terrible mistake that produced and amplified human suffering.

But it was also researchers, scientists, and academics who provided the data that led to the eventual removal of homosexuality from the *DSM* in 1973. The Kinsey studies of the 1940s and '50s found that homosexuality was far more prevalent in the general population than previously believed. Other researchers in the 1950s found that homosexuality occurs in all human societies and almost all animal species. Dr. Evelyn Hooker is credited with conducting the first empirical study comparing the mental health and social adjustment of gay men to straight men, published in 1956. The two groups in the study were, of course, indistinguishable—a shocking finding in the mid-twentieth century.[7] These and other scientific findings had far-reaching ramifications outside of the academic world, playing no small role in empowering the LGBTQ community to demand the rights and recognition they deserved.

While it's impossible to measure the overall research potential of humanity, here are a few statistics to give some sense of the amount of studying that people are engaging in at any one time: Each year, about a million people earn master's degrees from US universities alone, with millions more earning master's degrees in other countries. In addition, hundreds of thousands of doctoral degrees are awarded annually around the globe. The US has the most, with 55,700 doctoral graduates in 2019; Germany and the United Kingdom graduated close to 30,000 doctoral students.[8] That is a *lot* of time, effort, and brainpower being expended on research.

And it's certainly not just universities that engage in socially relevant research. There are more than 2,800 think tanks around the world.[9] There are also many research institutions, government agencies, nonprofits, and other types of organizations that have dedicated, skilled researchers closely examining societies' greatest challenges and proposing options for improvement. The amount of scholarship that is being generated about the human condition and the cultures and societies we occupy is staggering.

But not all the research being conducted is actually translating into tangible programs, policies, or decisions. Academia has, unfortunately, become increasingly siloed from other sectors and industries. Much of the wonderful research that's happening isn't reaching beyond the halls of universities or the pages of journals. We're often failing to implement the brilliant insights that the thinkers among us are discovering and naming.

According to environmental policy expert Dr. Asit Biswas and geography and environmental researcher Dr. Julian Kirchherr, academic research appears to be having a declining impact on public debates and policy development. "In the 1930s and 1940s, 20 per cent of articles in the prestigious *The American Political Science Review* focused on policy recommendations. At the last count, the share was down to a meagre 0.3 per cent," they explain. Published research papers have very little reach even within academia: "According to one estimate, only

20 per cent of papers cited have actually been read. We estimate that an average paper in a peer-reviewed journal is read completely by no more than 10 people."[10]

The problem, according to Biswas and Kirchherr, is the emphasis that universities and institutions the world over place on getting published in prestigious peer-reviewed journals. It is the ultimate crown jewel for professors and researchers, one that earns them jobs, salary increases, tenure, grants, staffing, and other benefits. These rewards come even if no one reads or is aware of their research. In contrast, there is little to be gained for scholars who submit an op-ed to a popular newspaper or magazine, or give presentations to the general public—except, perhaps, the derision of their peers for reaching out to the masses. As a result, many studies with important findings and conclusions simply gather dust on shelves or occupy obscure spaces online. This is to the detriment of all of us. A dearth of applicable, relevant scientific findings makes it that much harder to challenge existing injustices.

In the National Rifle Association's (NRA) efforts to promote the proliferation of guns in the United States, one of the organization's main strategies was to stifle research about gun violence. A landmark 1993 study had found that having a handgun at home nearly triples the chance that someone—usually a family member or friend—will be killed there. Shortly afterward, the NRA lobbied Congress to cut off government funding for any activity that might promote gun control.[11] The "Dickey Amendment," named after former Arkansas representative Jay Dickey, was enacted in 1996, and was remarkably effective at preventing government-funded gun research for twenty-three years. Without data-based evidence, the debate over gun control became dominated by an endless cycle of opinions, assertions, assumptions, and propaganda.

It wasn't until 2019, when the influence of the NRA began to wane and after the United States had seen hundreds of thousands of people killed by gun violence, that Congress restored funding for firearm injury prevention research. As of early 2021, the Centers for Disease Control and the National Institutes of Health were funding about two dozen different gun violence studies across the country.[12] Out of these studies could come practical, effective recommendations for policies and laws. While this alone isn't enough to address the epidemic of gun violence in the United States, it's a promising start.

Scholarship about the most pressing issues of our day can go from the realm of *interesting* to that of *world-changing* when it becomes more widely known and understood and leads to executable applications. "Academics can't operate in isolation from the world's very real problems," says Savo Heleta, manager of Internationalization at Home and Research at the Nelson Mandela University. "They may be producing important ideas and innovations that could help people understand and perhaps even begin to address issues like climate change, conflict, food insecurity and disease."[13]

Academic studies can even birth new movements. The field of environmental justice, or environmental racism, emerged from research. In 1979, sociologist Robert Bullard and his research team conducted a study of municipal waste disposal facilities in Houston, Texas, and found that the vast majority were located in Black neighborhoods, even though African Americans made up only a quarter of the city's population. This was the first comprehensive account of ecoracism in the United States, catalyzing a movement for environmental equity within the country.[14] It has now become a widely understood reality that "people who live, work and play in America's most polluted environments are commonly people of color and the poor"—but only because we have the unassailable facts to back that up.[15] When they are empowered with that knowledge, communities are better able to advocate for their rights.

Working in research may be appealing to highly sensitive individuals for a number of reasons. Sensitives love to learn. Much of the work is done alone or in small groups. It involves attention to detail, deep thinking, and finding meaning. There can be flexibility in pursuing your interests and creativity in designing studies. And it's an incredibly persuasive tool to encourage social change.

The world of research needs empathic professionals who will be conscientious in how they design and conduct studies; who will be inclusive of underrepresented groups and underrepresented issues; who will seek to connect their findings to real solutions that address real problems; who will intuitively sense how best to communicate results and recommendations to those who need to hear them.

Though they might spend much of their time in a laboratory or at a desk, researchers—like anyone who advocates for social change—aren't insulated from people, organizations, and forces that might oppose their work. It's no coincidence that oppressive regimes often target academics, professors, researchers, and scientists. Or that well-funded organizations with a vested interest in maintaining or expanding the status quo—like the NRA—would try to cut off resources for scientific research or academic fields of study. Or that lobbyists, politicians, commentators, social media influencers, and others would attack empirical research.

When your work proves that something is unjust and needs to be addressed, those who benefit from the status quo feel threatened. The knowledge of academics and researchers, shared among the populace, has great potential to foment social action.

"If what you do doesn't make a difference in the world, what good is it?" renowned computational mathematician C. K. "John" Chu once told then-graduate student Stephen Schneider.[16] Schneider went on to become one of the earliest scientists to sound the alarm about the possibility of climate change as far back as 1970. He was an internationally recognized climatologist and a tireless advocate for public education, debating skeptics and persuading policymakers until his death in 2010.

Schneider didn't shirk from contributing to newspapers and magazines or speaking at public events. He was disparaged by fellow scientists and politicians alike; he lost jobs and had his career threatened; he received hate mail, some of which verged on death threats, due to his research and his dogged determination to bring the risk of climate change before the public and decision-makers.[17] His 2009 memoir is fittingly called *Science as a Contact Sport: Inside the Battle to Save Earth's Climate.*

Conducting socially oriented research is not without risks, but the potential impact is immense. We need academics who can help identify how our systems are failing and who is being hurt as a result. We need researchers who can untangle the root causes of oppression and inequality. We need deep thinkers who can analyze societal challenges and propose policies and programs to create change, as well as empathic communicators who can distill the science into powerful messaging for the public. Knowledge, as we know, is power—especially when intuitive, thoughtful minds are asking the most important questions and persevering in their pursuit of the answers that our societies need to know.

Our history books have already been altered by the connectors, creatives, record keepers, builders, equippers, and researchers who have come before us. Sensitive, empathic justice seekers have led, discovered, and supported in all of these fields—and in many more. Their stories, vocations, and callings are only a small sample of the paths through which each of us can contribute to the social good.

Their paths might be yours, might cross yours, or be far from yours. But we are because they are, and they are because we are. If we open our hearts, we may find that the seeds of possibility can take root.

18

The Integrity of You

> "Not everything that is faced can be changed,
> but nothing can be changed until it is faced."
>
> James Baldwin

Are you listening? What *are your mind, heart, body, and spirit telling you?*

When, as a young adult, I first felt that spark of passion to pursue social justice, I remember being full of hope. Full of excitement. Full of ideas and possibilities.

And then reality hit. The work was arduous, the impact imperceptible. Some of the people I encountered were wonderful; others were decidedly unpleasant. The social issues I wanted to help solve were far more complex and deeply entrenched than I had ever imagined. Over the years, it became increasingly easy to give in to discouragement and to listen to cynicism. I spent far more time wallowing in despair than I care to admit.

But I am just beginning to understand, more than two decades later, that I spent most of my adulthood chasing a version of myself that didn't exist. I wanted so desperately to live up to the Activist Ideal. At some points in my life, I think I would have sacrificed almost anything to become the kind of fearless, decisive, confident social justice leader that I had always envisioned.

Yet in sacrificing my authentic self—with all my gifts and limitations, my strengths and challenges—I also hurt my ability to contribute meaningfully to causes. After burning out multiple times and spending years recovering from each burnout, I was no closer to the Activist Ideal than I had been to begin with. I was simply a more wounded and exhausted version of who I had always been.

For those of us committed to walking this road of social justice for the long run, we need to trade our well-intentioned but misguided idealism for a cohesive and authentic integrity. Who you are is who you live as. Your choices and actions are consistent with your characteristics, interests, gifts, traits, skills, and sensitivities.

So, it starts with me. It starts with you.

Who are you, really? And are you willing to embrace that person, to nurture that person, to value their well-being as much as you do another's? For it is in health, in groundedness, in authenticity, in gratitude, and, yes, even in joy, that we can be the most effective agent for positive social change. When we are doing what we were meant to do with the best of what we have, we can experience a deep sense of rightness, of soul contentment.

"If we are to live our lives fully and well," says Parker Palmer, "we must learn to embrace the opposites, to live in a creative tension between our limits and our potentials."[1] Some of your limits and your potentials will be defined by your experience of sensitivity, empathy, or introversion. The sensitive soul sees and ponders things that others don't. The empathic individual experiences the world in a way that many cannot understand. The deeply introverted person is a particular kind of person with particular needs. These are the wonderfully complex traits that we embody. And, in a world dominated by the aggressive and assertive, these are the traits we are meant to proudly and earnestly bring into the social justice arena.

To be a sensitive, empathic soul engaged in social justice is not an easy calling by any measure. The pain—emotional, physical, and spiritual—we experience as we engage with suffering, oppression, poverty, and injustice is real. It can be searing. If you let it, it can knock you down. And it will hurt. But hopefully, after dusting yourself off, you can find a way to keep getting up and walking forward, empowered with greater understanding for who you are and your place in the story of positive social progress.

Everything we've looked at together in this book—the details of personalities and the logistics of social justice work, the pursuit of calling and the finding of your particular place—only matters if we also maintain hope. Without hope, we will not do the hard work of understanding ourselves, other people, organizations, and movements. We will not persevere when we experience disappointment or failure. We will not keep looking for that particular activity or role or issue area that makes our hearts sing. Social justice work is hard; the effort to find where you fit within social justice is also hard. Hope is the fuel we need to continue forward.

For me, hope does not spring organically. I do not have a hope-generator built within me. I suspect many other highly sensitive people are the same. We notice too many details of pain and suffering; we feel the anger and despair of many around us. Any natural wellspring of hope we may have carried is gradually drained by the negative circumstances of our world.

Fortunately, hope is a choice. It is a verb, an action that we pursue. "This is the shadow of hope. Knowing that we may never see the realization of our dreams, and yet still showing up," writes Austin Channing Brown in her book *I'm Still Here: Black Dignity in a World Made for Whiteness.*[2]

And when the fuse of hope is lit in our lives, far more possibilities for goodness and change open up. As Buddhist philosopher and nuclear disarmament advocate Daisaku Ikeda writes, "Hope changes everything, starting with our lives. Hope is the force that enables us to take action to make our dreams come true. It has the power to change winter into summer, barrenness to creativity, agony to joy."[3]

We can choose to embrace this force each day rather than give in to the despairing voices around us. We can choose to practice gratitude, to do what gives us joy, to study best practices, to surround ourselves with wise and encouraging people. We can choose to believe that we are doing enough. That we *are* enough. This doesn't mean that we turn away from the hardships of the world. But we pay attention to both the hard and the hopeful, and in so doing, we grow to be wiser, stronger people.

Hope within the sensitive soul is something to behold. I believe it is a particularly potent force. This hope is not abstract and aimless; rather, it is measured and thoughtful, compassionate and directed. Hopeful sensitives have the tools and the energy to create specific, implementable plans and visions for themselves and for the greater good of their communities. They will always keep human beings at the core of their actions and choices.

By cultivating more hope within ourselves, even when we are not *feeling* particularly hopeful, we are far more likely to find callings within social justice that are a wonderful fit for our personality, talents, interests, and skills. We are far more likely to find the friends, partners, and allies we need along the way.

The world needs sensitive empaths in the arena, highlighting injustices, promoting equity, and creating solutions. But the world also needs sensitives who want to be there and are able to be there for what will inevitably be a long fight.

The particular mix of gifts, traits, interests, and passions that makes you so unique will undoubtedly lead you to unexpected places, unknown places, unrecognizable places. You may find yourself advocating for the social good in unusual ways. If so, you may very well have found exactly what you were meant to do.

No matter where your individual journey takes you, I hope you'll stay engaged in working for the social good—if not in the arena itself, at least on the outskirts or on the support team. The fight for social justice is ugly these days. We live in a time of anger, of confrontation, of deep divisions, of distorted realities. The warrior kings, on every side of every social issue, are running amok. We need priestly advisers to remind us of our shared humanity. Of our ability to connect and love. Of our potential for good. Effective social advocacy and lasting social change require gentleness, nonviolence, empathy, collaboration, and creativity.

It's a big ask. But this isn't your burden to bear alone. You are one in a long, rich tradition of change makers—some whose names we know and many whose names we don't know. There are many others on this planet right now who care deeply about the flourishing of all humanity, and there will be many more who come after you. It is not your responsibility to save the world. It is, however, your responsibility to be the best, most authentic version of yourself that you know to be, and, when you are able and ready, to let the rest of us revel in the goodness that you have to offer.

When the sensitive and empathic among us are able to find themselves and share that for the sake of humanity, I believe the world can't help but become a little more bright and beauteous.

Acknowledgments

The idea and title for this book suddenly popped into my head as I was walking along the trail near my home and pondering the question, "If I were to write another book, what would I write about?" As soon as the idea came to me, I felt a resounding *Yes* in my soul. But I was only asking this question of myself because Lil Copan, editor extraordinaire, had asked it of me first.

This was my first experience working with a book editor from preconcept all the way to publication. It was a joy and a privilege to be advised, encouraged, and cheered on throughout the process by such a wise, dedicated soul. Thank you for all you have given to this book and to me, Lil.

And thank you to Pete Feely, Alyssa Miller, Elle Rogers, Jana Nelson, and the rest of the wonderful team at Broadleaf, who rocked the editorial process, designed a beautiful cover and layout, and provided generous, authentic marketing support.

To the friends, old and new, who offered their endorsements and generous support for this book: I am deeply grateful. Knowing that I have such accomplished, genuine, well-respected thought leaders, activists, and authors in my corner means so much to me.

I'm immensely grateful for the writer friends who have been my community throughout this journey. In particular, many thanks to Cara Meredith and Anna Broadway for reviewing and giving such helpful feedback on my book proposal. Thank you also to fellow highly sensitive person Heather Caliri, who passed along several helpful ideas and anecdotes that contributed to the manuscript. I'm also grateful to be part of the fabulous Redbud Writers Guild and other informal writers' networks. Many of you helped share my survey, connect me to resources, and continue to teach me about this peculiar writing life—thank you.

The research in this book would not have been possible without the uber-smart academics in my life. I'm grateful to my big sister, Dr. Karen Cheng-Ramos, who first introduced me to the concept of highly sensitive people and reviewed my survey to ensure that it met social science research standards. Thank you also to Dr. Chris Smallwood for his assistance connecting me to journals and research papers.

My very best experiences in the social justice arena have always taken place alongside talented, committed, courageous individuals with incredible hearts. These are the people reshaping communities around the world, and they have played a significant role in my own transformation. I'm not able to name everyone, but here are some of the wonderful people I have had the privilege of collaborating with over the years and who continue to inspire me and give me hope: Angela, Brad, Cari, Chris, Dana, Drew, Duane, Eli, Erica, Ernest, Gabe, Greg, Jai, Janet, Jim, Joanna, Josh, Josue, Kristina, Lisa, Mario, Marisa, Michelle, Mike, Mondo, Nadinne, Omowale, Osheta, Patricia, Ray, Sam, Sandy, Su, and Xian. I am because you are.

To my River small group: You have been a lifeline to me through the pandemic and all the ups and downs of the past few years. Thank you for your many prayers and words of encouragement as I labored to finish this book. Through you, I clearly see the image of a good, gracious, and loving God.

This book would never have happened without a duo of incredible grandmas who regularly helped watch the kids and gave me much-needed breaks. Much love and gratitude to both of you.

And to Ned, the love of my life, thanks for your unfailing faith in me. You continue to nudge me toward making brave, authentic choices, even when I don't feel like doing so. Jonah and Isaac, thank you for *sometimes* letting me write. Watching you become who you are meant to be is the most profound experience of my life. You give me so much hope for the future.

APPENDIX

Your Uniquely Sensitive Self

"When I discover who I am, I'll be free."

Ralph Ellison

Every five years or so, I arrive at a place where I feel fairly confident in my understanding of myself. I've done the work: reflected deeply, talked to a therapist, journaled, read books, completed exercises, talked to wise friends, watched TED talks, and even received the occasional divinely inspired insight. I think I understand what makes me tick, what I should work on, how I've been impacted by trauma, where my tender spots remain, what I need, why I need it, and how to ask for it. I've got a good handle on who I am and where I'm going. Until I don't.

In the face of major life events, my previous self-perceptions often evaporate. I learn to see myself in totally different ways. Sometimes I encounter different models of psychology or personality; other times I receive a particularly profound insight from someone else.

The heart and mind of every individual human being are cavernous, complex, evolving vessels that require perpetual excavation. The heart and mind of the sensitive human being even more so, with the extra levels of observing, sensing, absorbing, processing, thinking, and reflecting that we tend to do. Working to understand ourselves is an ongoing and challenging but ultimately rewarding lifelong journey.

Among those of us who identify as highly sensitive or empathic, there is no simple formula for explaining who you are or what kind of social justice-oriented activity fits you. We are each sensitive in our own particular way. As Dr. Elaine Aron explains, "This may be due to there being several different causes of the trait, leading to different kinds, or 'flavors,' of sensitivity, some of them stronger than others, or to some people being born with two kinds, three kinds, and so on."[1] How we're sensitive, why we're sensitive, and what we're sensitive to can all vary considerably.

On top of that, we each have dozens, if not hundreds, of other traits and characteristics that will impact what we feel, how we feel it, and how it gets expressed. To have some idea of the kind of social cause, activism, or role that would be the best fit for you, it's worth taking the time to get to know yourself in all your unique, complicated, nuanced glory. Self-awareness is self-empowerment. It is an essential step toward finding the kind of work, service, or activity that fits your spirit and nourishes your soul and will help point you toward overall health, balance, and contentment.

While we can't explore every part of your personality here, the following are four of the most significant traits that tend to impact an individual's "flavor" of sensitivity and empathy. I hope you will take some time to explore these and reflect, journal, talk to a friend, or engage in other helpful practices—to consider who you are in this moment in your life. This may not be who you are in a few years, months, or even weeks, so consider revisiting this appendix or other helpful tools when your emotional currents have shifted or the map of your neural pathways has altered.

Sensory Sensitivities

Sensitive people tend to have sensory experiences that are more intense than that of their nonsensitive peers. Of the five primary senses—sight, smell, taste, hearing, and touch—you may experience particular sensitivity with some of these more than others. So, consider these questions to help you reflect on your own sensory sensitivities:

- In which of the five senses do you experience more sensitivity? Which senses are less sensitive? (You might want to rank them from 1 to 5, where 1 is most sensitive and 5 is least sensitive.)
- What kinds of environments, especially those you might find yourself in while engaging in social justice work (an office, a protest, a community meeting, etc.), are the most comfortable for you? What kind of environments are more difficult to tolerate?
- What kind of activities have nurtured your senses in a positive way? What activities have overwhelmed your senses?
- What sort of colleagues or organizational culture appeal to your senses? Which are challenging?

Introverts versus Extroverts

As many as 70 percent of sensitive individuals are introverts. The two characteristics go hand in hand, as people oftentimes create the contexts that overwhelm us. People can be the cause of noise, reduced physical space, emotion, pain, conflict, pressure, threats, and more. The typical sensitive introvert will prefer having plenty of alone time and being in smaller groups or one on one.

In contrast, the sensitive extrovert, like any other extrovert, tends to have large numbers of friends, enjoys being in groups, and appreciates meeting strangers. More often than not, being around people is not what will overstimulate the extroverted highly sensitive person. But there are still plenty of other circumstances that could cause an outgoing sensitive to feel overwhelmed, like work, conflict, or other stress. Once overwhelmed, the extrovert will likely need to withdraw from people and crowds to find calm and quiet.

Of course, no one is wholly introverted or wholly extroverted. Even the most deeply introverted person will enjoy being around people (or a person) occasionally; likewise, the most extreme extrovert needs occasional solitude.

Whether you are introverted or extroverted, here are some things to think about as you consider where you fit in the social justice arena:

- What size groups are you most comfortable in or energized by? At what size do groups begin to exhaust you? How much time do you think you could comfortably spend in a group setting in a day or a week?
- If you had to work with someone regularly (like a boss, teammate, partner, or direct report), what kinds of characteristics would give you energy? What traits would take energy away from you?
- What is your tolerance level for spending time with people who have trauma, mental illness, addictions, or other struggles that might affect their behavior and the feelings they emote?

High Sensation Seekers

There is a subset of sensitive people who prioritize intentionally seeking novel and stimulating experiences. Researchers have found that our brains have two separate systems: the "behavioral activation system," which takes in information and moves us toward things, especially new things, and the "behavioral inhibition system," which focuses on perceived threats and dangers and nudges us away from those things.

Sensitives tend to have a balance between both systems, but the strength of those systems can differ substantially. Individuals with more muted behavioral activation and behavioral inhibition systems will likely be quieter and calmer, with a tendency to settle into predictable patterns of life. Those that have more active systems will experience a more dramatic push-and-pull between wanting to try new things and being overwhelmed by them. "This kind of HSP would be both very curious and very cautious, bold yet anxious, easily bored yet easily overaroused," explains Dr. Aron.[2]

For the high sensation seeker (HSS), the ideal job or volunteer role encompasses a variety of activities. The responsibilities grow with you, providing new levels of interest and challenge. When new skills have been mastered, high attention seekers might experience boredom and, eventually, burnout.

If you answer yes to all or most of the questions that follow, you are probably a high sensation seeker. Being aware of this characteristic will help you grow your awareness in finding that optimal level of excitement and novelty.

- Do you often find yourself restless for newness, whether it's a new experience or something new to learn or think about?
- Do you tend to push yourself into trying novel things even when you know they will probably tire you out?
- Do you tend to overcommit, taking on more than you can actually do?
- Do you sometimes have trouble finishing an activity or commitment because you were distracted by something new and different?

Types of Empaths

Like highly sensitive people, empathic people come in many forms, and what they are particularly attuned to can differ dramatically. *Empathy* has been closely studied by scientists and academics; *empaths*, not so much. But psychologists acknowledge that there are multiple types of empaths who absorb different emotions and sensations from different things or beings. In her book, *The Happy Empath: A Survival Guide for Highly Sensitive People*, certified life coach and empath Christine Rose Elle names eight different types of empaths:

1. **Emotional empaths** feel others' emotions. This is the most common understanding of what it means to be an empath.
2. **Physical empaths** intuit the physical sensations that others are experiencing or may even experience those sensations themselves.
3. **Energy empaths** are able to form a complex, holistic impression of another person through their heightened senses.
4. **Plant empaths** connect deeply with plants, trees, and other living organisms, and understand what they need.
5. **Animal empaths** bond strongly with creatures, sensing their needs and feelings. They may also be particularly attuned to the physical cues of emotion—facial expressions, gestures, and so on—that humans give.
6. **Intuitive empaths** have the ability to notice even the most subtle bits of information about a person through their five senses, giving them the ability to deeply understand and even possibly predict another's behaviors.
7. **Aesthetic empaths** connect with the emotion and meaning of works of art, including film, visual art,

literature, and more. They can sense better than most what the creator of the piece wants to communicate.

8. **Environmental empaths** are very aware of the atmosphere and the details of places, both in the natural world and in built environments like homes, schools, and offices. They may be particularly sensitive to loud, crowded, and chaotic places.[3]

If you identify as an empath, then understanding what kind of empath you are will give you important clues as to what social issues may be of most concern to you, as well as the kind of interactions that might drain you the most. You might also identify as more than one type of empath, or you may be keenly empathic in one way but only moderately so in another way. Here are some questions to begin to process what kind of empath you might be:

- When you are around people, what, if anything, do you tend to absorb from them: emotions, physical sensations, sensory inputs, energy, or something else?
- How connected do you tend to feel to nature and natural beings, such as animals and plants? Do your emotions and thoughts change significantly when you spend time in nature or with plants or animals?
- When you are in different environments, how do you gauge the vibe of the place? Is it from the people, the way it's designed, the aesthetics, or something else?
- Of all the different things above that affect you, which affect you the most? Which do you carry with you for the longest?

Additional Resources

There are many other books, tools, and resources we can turn to in order to better understand ourselves and how we operate as sensitive, empathic, or introverted individuals, including:

- *The Highly Sensitive Person: How to Thrive When the World Overwhelms You* by Dr. Elaine Aron
- *The Highly Sensitive Parent: Be Brilliant in Your Role, Even When the World Overwhelms You* by Dr. Elaine Aron
- The Highly Sensitive Person website (includes assessment and articles): hsperson.com
- The Highly Sensitive Refuge website (includes many articles): highlysensitiverefuge.com
- *Quiet: The Power of Introverts in a World that Can't Stop Talking* by Susan Cain
- *Bittersweet: How Sorrow and Longing Make Us Whole* by Susan Cain
- *The Empath's Survival Guide: Life Strategies for Sensitive People* by Judith Orloff
- *The Happy Empath: A Survival Guide for Highly Sensitive People* by Christine Rose Elle
- *The Gifts of Imperfection: Let Go of Who You Think You're Supposed to Be and Embrace Who You Are* by Brené Brown
- *Rising Strong: How the Ability to Reset Transforms the Way We Love, Live, Parent, and Lead* by Brené Brown
- *The Wisdom of the Enneagram: The Complete Guide to Psychological and Spiritual Growth for the Nine Personality Types* by Don Richard Riso and Russ Hudson
- *The Enneagram: A Christian Perspective* by Richard Rohr and Andreas Ebert
- The Myers & Briggs Foundation website (includes the MBTI assessment): myersbriggs.org
- DiSC Profile website (includes detailed descriptions of the DiSC styles): discprofile.com
- The Birkman Method website (includes detailed descriptions of key perspectives and motivations): Birkman.com

For more career-oriented wisdom, you may want to look at:

- *Making Work Work for the Highly Sensitive Person: Learning to Bend, Not Break, When Work Overwhelms You* by Barrie Jaeger
- *Designing Your Life: Build the Perfect Career, Step by Step* by Bill Burnett and Dave Evans
- *Let Your Life Speak: Listening for the Voice of Vocation* by Parker Palmer
- *The Lightmaker's Manifesto: How to Work for Change without Losing Your Joy* by Karen Walrond
- *What Color Is Your Parachute? Your Guide to a Lifetime of Meaningful Work and Career Success* by Richard N. Bolles (updated annually)
- *The Pathfinder: How to Choose or Change Your Career for a Lifetime of Satisfaction and Success* by Nicholas Lore

If you'd like some inspiration, especially on how to engage in social justice creatively, contemplatively, compassionately, and authentically, here are some wonderful resources:

- *Gandhi: An Autobiography: The Story of My Experiments with Truth* by Mahatma Gandhi
- *My Life with Martin Luther King, Jr.* by Coretta Scott King
- *The Fire Within* by James Baldwin
- *Meditations of the Heart* by Howard Thurman
- *The Collected Poems of Langston Hughes*, edited by Arnold Rampersad
- *The Book of Forgiving: The Fourfold Path for Healing Ourselves and Our World* by Desmond Tutu and Mpho Tutu
- *Long Walk to Freedom: The Autobiography of Nelson Mandela* by Nelson Mandela
- *Being Peace* by Thich Nhat Hanh

- *Mountains beyond Mountains: The Quest of Dr. Paul Farmer, a Man Who Would Cure the World* by Tracy Kidder
- *A People's Art History of the United States: 250 Years of Activist Art and Artists Working in Social Justice Movements* by Nicolas Lampert
- *Out of Poverty: What Works When Traditional Approaches Fail* by Paul Polak
- *How to Change the World: Social Entrepreneurs and the Power of New Ideas* by David Bornstein
- *Manifesto for a Moral Revolution: Practices to Build a Better World* by Jacqueline Novogratz
- *Dear White Peacemakers: Dismantling Racism with Grit and Grace* by Osheta Moore
- *Becoming Rooted: One Hundred Days of Becoming Connected with Sacred Earth* by Randy Woodley
- *Be the Bridge: Pursuing God's Heart for Racial Reconciliation* by Latasha Morrison
- *Bread for the Resistance: 40 Devotions for Justice People* by Donna Barber
- Center for Action and Contemplation website

Notes

Introduction

1 Mahatma Gandhi, *Gandhi: An Autobiography: The Story of My Experiments with Truth* (Boston: Beacon, 1993), 59.

2 Gandhi, *Gandhi: An Autobiography*, 62.

3 Jenn Granneman, "Are You Highly Sensitive? {Take the Highly Sensitive Person Test}," *Introvert, Dear,* July 8, 2015, accessed March 29, 2021, https://introvertdear.com/news/highly-sensitive-person-test-quiz/.

4 Elaine N. Aron, *The Highly Sensitive Person: How to Thrive When the World Overwhelms You* (New York: Harmony, 2016), xvii–xxi.

5 "Mahatma Gandhi," Biography.com, published April 27, 2017, updated August 20, 2019, accessed March 29, 2021, https://www.biography.com/activist/mahatma-gandhi.

6 "Matahma Gandhi."

7 Michael Pluess, "Here's Everything Researchers Know about High Sensitivity, as of 2021," *Highly Sensitive Refuge*, November 26, 2021, accessed July 20, 2022, https://highlysensitiverefuge.com/heres-everything-researchers-know-about-high-sensitivity-as-of-2021/.

8 Melody Wilding, "Why Highly Sensitive People Make the Best Leaders, According to a Psychologist," *Forbes*, April 13, 2020, accessed March 25, 2021, https://www.forbes.com/sites/melodywilding/2020/04/13/why-highly-sensitive-people-make-the-best-leaders-according-to-a-psychologist/?sh=4705d4235db9.

9 Hannah Ewens, "Super Empaths Are Real, Study Finds," *Motherboard: Tech by Vice*, November 8, 2018, accessed March 25, 2021, https://www. vice.com /en/article/xwj84k/super-empaths-are-real-says-study.

10 Susan Cain, *Quiet: The Power of Introverts in World that Won't Stop Talking* (New York: Crown, 2012), 10.

11 Erica Sloan, "Are You Truly an Introvert . . . or Actually a Highly Sensitive Person?" *Well + Good*, July 11, 2022, accessed September 13, 2022, https:// www.wellandgood.com/introvert-versus-sensitive-person/.

12 "Sensory Processing Sensitivity," *Wikipedia*, accessed March 25, 2021, https:// en.wikipedia.org/wiki/Sensory_processing_sensitivity.

13 Aron, *Highly Sensitive Person*, xv.

14 Vidya Hattangadi, "Why Highly Sensitive People Are a Boon to Humanity," *Financial Express*, October 28, 2019, accessed March 27, 2021, https://www. financialexpress.com/opinion/why-highly-sensitive-people-are-a-boon-to -humanity/1747378/.

15 "Social Justice," Oxford Reference, accessed March 27, 2021, https://www .oxfordreference.com/view/10.1093/oi/authority.20110803100515279.

16 Emmaline Soken-Huberty, "What Does Social Justice Mean?" Human Rights Careers, accessed March 27, 2021, https://www.humanrightscareers .com/issues/what-does-social-justice-mean/.

Chapter 1

1 Barrie Jaeger, *Making Work Work for the Highly Sensitive Person: Learning to Bend, Not Break, When Work Overwhelms You* (New York: McGraw-Hill, 2004), 52.

2 Aron, *Highly Sensitive Person*, 28.

3 Jonathan Timm, "The Plight of the Overworked Nonprofit Employee," *Atlantic*, August 24, 2016, accessed February 23, 2022, https://www.theat lantic.com/business/archive/2016/08/the-plight-of-the-overworked-non profit-employee/497081/.

4 Chris Strub, "45% of Nonprofit Employees to Seek New Jobs By 2025: Report," *Forbes*, February 10, 2020, accessed February 23, 2022, https://www .forbes.com/sites/chrisstrub/2020/02/10/nonprofithr/?sh=4fa9e29a15ca.

5 Emily Nagoski and Amelia Nagoski, *Burnout: The Secret to Unlocking the Stress Cycle* (New York: Ballantine, 2019), xi.

6 Bessel van den Kolk, *The Body Keeps the Score: Brain, Mind, and Body in the Healing of Trauma* (New York: Penguin, 2014), 2.

7 Sam Farmer, "How Greta Thunberg's Autism Helped Make Her the World's Most Important Person for 2020," *Hill*, December 12, 2019, accessed February 23, 2022, https://thehill.com/changing-america/well-being/468091 -opinion-activist-greta-thunbergs-autism-doesnt-hold-her-back.

8 Rebecca Rowell, *Malala Yousafzai: Education Activist* (North Mankato, MN: ABDO, 2014), 53.

9 Aron, *Highly Sensitive Person*, 37.

10 Aron, *Highly Sensitive Person*, 52.

Chapter 2

1 Elaine N. Aron, *The Highly Sensitive Person: How to Thrive When the World Overwhelms You* (New York: Harmony, 2016), 18.
2 Aron, *Highly Sensitive Person,* 20.
3 Susan Cain, *Quiet: The Power of Introverts in a World That Won't Stop Talking* (New York: Crown, 2012), 4–5.
4 Pankaj Mishra, *Age of Anger: A History of the Present* (New York: Farrar, Straus and Giroux, 2017).
5 Pankaj Mishra, "Welcome to the Age of Anger," *The Guardian*, December 8, 2016, accessed November 17, 2021, https://www.theguardian.com/politics/2016/dec/08/welcome-age-anger-brexit-trump.
6 Kathleen Rodgers, "'Anger Is Why We're All Here': Mobilizing and Managing Emotions in a Professional Activist Organization," *Social Movement Studies* 9, no. 3 (2010), 273–91.
7 Katherine Ellison, "Five Things Worth Knowing about Empathy," *Washington Post,* January 17, 2021, accessed November 20, 2021, https://www.washingtonpost.com/health/empathy-what-to-know/2021/01/15/b3c7665c-4ea4-11eb-bda4-615aaefd0555_story.html.
8 Zurich Insurance Group, "Decline in Global Empathy Creates Global Risks in the 'Age of Anger,'" April 8, 2019, accessed November 20, 2021, https://www.zurich.com/en/knowledge/topics/global-risks/decline-human-empathy-creates-global-risks-age-of-anger.
9 Emma Sepälä, "Empathy Is on the Decline in This Country. A New Book Describes What We Can Do to Bring It Back," *Washington Post*, June 11, 2019, accessed November 21, 2021, https://www.washingtonpost.com/lifestyle/2019/06/11/empathy-is-decline-this-country-new-book-describes-what-we-can-do-bring-it-back/.
10 Tim Craig, "U.S. Political Divide Becomes Increasingly Violent, Rattling Activists and Police," *Washington Post*, August 27, 2020, accessed November 21, 2021, https://www.washingtonpost.com/national/protests-violence/2020/08/27/3f232e66-e578-11ea-970a-64c73a1c2392_story.html.
11 Michael O. Schroeder, "The Physical and Mental Toll of Being Angry All the Time," *U.S. News & World Report*, October 26, 2017, accessed November 30, 2021, https://health.usnews.com/wellness/mind/articles/2017-10-26/the-physical-and-mental-toll-of-being-angry-all-the-time.
12 Elizabeth Kolbert, "Why Facts Don't Change Our Minds," *New Yorker*, February 27, 2017, accessed December 5, 2021, https://www.newyorker.com/magazine/2017/02/27/why-facts-dont-change-our-minds.
13 Sahara Byrne and Philip Solomon Hart, "The Boomerang Effect: A Synthesis of Findings and a Preliminary Theoretical Framework," *Annals of the International Communication Association* 33, no. 1 (2009), 3–37.
14 David Robson, "The '3.5% Rule': How a Small Minority Can Change the World," *BBC Future*, May 13, 2019, accessed June 15, 2022, https://www.bbc.com/future/article/20190513-it-only-takes-35-of-people-to-change-the-world.

15 Roderick Matthews, "Friends and Enemies: An Excerpt from Roderick Matthews' Book 'Jinnah vs. Gandhi'," *Hindu*, August 11, 2012, updated August 20, 2012, accessed December 18, 2021, https://www.thehindu.com/books/friends-and-enemies-an-excerpt-from-roderick-matthews-book-jinnah-vs-gandhi/article12689070.ece.

16 The King Center, "The King Philosophy—Nonviolence 365," accessed January 21, 2022, https://thekingcenter.org/about-tkc/the-king-philosophy/.

17 James M. Washington, ed., *A Testament of Hope: The Essential Writings and Speeches of Martin Luther King, Jr.* (San Francisco: HarperCollins, 1991), 289, 302.

18 The King Center, "King Philosophy."

19 Martin Luther King Jr., "Statement to the Press at the Beginning of the Youth Leadership Conference," Raleigh, NC, April 15, 1960, accessed December 5, 2021, https://kinginstitute.stanford.edu/king-papers/documents/statement-press-beginning-youth-leadership-conference.

20 adrienne marie brown, *Emergent Strategy: Shaping Change, Changing Worlds* (Chico, CA: AK Press, 2017), 12.

21 brown, *Emergent Strategy*, 14.

22 "Theory of Enchantment," accessed July 26, 2022, https://theory-of-enchantment.teachable.com/p/theory-of-enchantment-homepage.

Chapter 3

1 "Star Trek's Uhura Reflects on MLK Encounter," *Tell Me More*, NPR, January 17, 2011, accessed September 16, 2021, https://www.npr.org/2011/01/17/132942461/Star-Treks-Uhura-Reflects-On-MLK-Encounter.

2 "Nichelle Nichols," *Wikipedia*, accessed September 16, 2021, https://en.wikipedia.org/wiki/Nichelle_Nichols.

3 History.com editors, "Loving v. Virginia," History.com, November 17, 2017, updated January 25, 2021, accessed September 30, 2021, https://www.history.com/topics/civil-rights-movement/loving-v-virginia.

4 "Nichelle Nichols."

5 Camille Jackson, "The Legacy of Lt. Uhura: Astronaut Mae Jemison on Race in Space," *Duke Today*, October 28, 2013, accessed September 16, 2021, https://today.duke.edu/2013/10/maejemison. See also Edward Moyer, "'Star Trek' in the White House: Obama and Uhura go Vulcan," *CNET*, April 4, 2012, accessed September 16, 2021, https://www.cnet.com/news/star-trek-in-the-white-house-obama-and-uhura-go-vulcan/.

6 Emma Craddock, "Living against Austerity: A Feminist Investigation of Doing Activism and Being Activist," *Policy Press Scholarship Online*, March 2020, accessed September 12, 2022, https://policypress.universitypressscholarship.com/view/10.1332/policypress/9781529205701.001.0001/upso-9781529205701-chapter-006.

7 Susan Cain, *Quiet: The Power of Introverts in a World That Won't Stop Talking* (New York: Crown, 2012), 4.

8 Laura Sanders, "Rare Brain Disorder Prevents All Fear," Science News, *Wired*, December 16, 2010, accessed September 28, 2021, https://www.wired.com/2010/12/fear-brain-amygdala/.

9 Weixia Chen and Paul C. Gorski, "Burnout in Social Justice and Human Rights Activists: Symptoms, Causes and Implications," *Journal of Human Rights Practice* 7, no. 3 (2015), 1–25.

10 Chen and Gorski, "Burnout in Social Justice and Human Rights Activists," 3.

11 Chen and Gorski, "Burnout in Social Justice and Human Rights Activists," 16–17.

12 Jen Plyler, "How to Keep on Keeping On: Sustaining Ourselves in Community Organizing and Social Justice Struggles," *Upping the Anti* 3, October 26, 2009, accessed September 13, 2022, https://uppingtheanti.org/journal/article/03-how-to-keep-on-keeping-on/.

13 Kristin Neff, "Four Ways Self-Compassion Can Help You Fight for Social Justice," *Greater Good Magazine*, June 14, 2021, accessed October 11, 2021, https://greatergood.berkeley.edu/article/item/four_ways_self_compassion_can_help_you_fight_for_social_justice.

14 Brené Brown, "Comparative Suffering, the 50/50 Myth, and Settling the Ball," *Unlocking Us* (podcast), March 27, 2020, accessed October 11, 2021, https://brenebrown.com/podcast/brene-on-comparative-suffering-the-50-50-myth-and-settling-the-ball/.

Chapter 4

1 Kirstin Downey, *The Woman behind the New Deal: The Life of Frances Perkins, FDR's Secretary of Labor and His Moral Conscience* (New York: Nan A. Talese, 2009), 2.

2 Downey, *The Woman behind the New Deal*, 1.

3 Downey, *The Woman behind the New Deal*, 336–73.

4 Downey, *The Woman behind the New Deal*, 347–48.

5 "Resilience," *Merriam-Webster Online Dictionary*, accessed October 19, 2021, https://www.merriam-webster.com/dictionary/resilience.

6 Andrew Zolli, *Resilience: Why Things Bounce Back* (New York: Simon & Schuster, 2012), 7.

7 Zolli, *Resilience*, 8.

8 American Psychological Association, "Building Your Resilience," January 1, 2012, updated February 1, 2020, accessed October 21, 2021, https://www.apa.org/topics/resilience.

9 Martin Brokenleg, "Transforming Cultural Trauma into Resilience," *Reclaiming Children and Youth* 21, no. 3 (Fall 2012), 12, accessed October 21, 2021, http://martinbrokenleg.com/wp-content/uploads/2016/02/21_3_Brokenleg.pdf.

10 Brené Brown, *Rising Strong: How the Ability to Reset Transforms the Way We Live, Love, Parent, and Lead* (New York: Random House, 2017), 10.

11 Rick Hanson and Forrest Hanson, *Resilient: How to Grow an Unshakable Core of Calm, Strength, and Happiness* (New York: Harmony, 2018), 1.

12 Jared E. Alcántara, *The Practices of Christian Preaching: Essentials for Effective Proclamation* (Grand Rapids, MI: Baker, 2019), 63.

13 Robert D. McFadden, "Vinoba Bhave, A Gandhi Disciple and Social Reformer, Dies at 87," *New York Times*, Section D, 25, November 16, 1982, accessed December 18, 2021, nytimes.com/1982/11/16/obituaries/vinoba-bhave-a-gandhi-disciple-and-social-reformer-dies-at-87.html.

14 "Yerkes-Dodson Law," *Wikipedia*, accessed September 22, 2021, https://en.wikipedia.org/wiki/Yerkes%E2%80%93Dodson_law.

15 Juliette Tocino-Smith, "What Is Eustress and How Is It Different from Stress?" *PositivePsychology.com*, October 12, 2021, accessed December 13, 2021, https://positivepsychology.com/what-is-eustress/.

16 Tocino-Smith, "What Is Eustress and How Is It Different from Stress?"

17 "Yerkes-Dodson Law," *Wikipedia.*

18 Brown, *Rising Strong*, 40–41.

19 Bessel van den Kolk, *The Body Keeps the Score: Brain, Mind, and Body in the Healing of Trauma* (New York: Penguin, 2014), 1.

20 James Baldwin, *The Fire Next Time* (New York: Vintage, 1993), 27.

Chapter 5

1 Nelson Mandela, *The Struggle Is My Life* (New York: Pathfinder, 1990), 14–28.

2 History.com editors, "Nelson Mandela Released from Prison," History.com, February 9, 2010, updated February 9, 2021, accessed December 4, 2021, https://www.history.com/this-day-in-history/nelson-mandela-released-from-prison.

3 Raymond Suttner, "Nelson Mandela's Leadership: His 'Obstinacy and Stubbornness' (Part 2)," *Daily Maverick*, June 11, 2018, accessed December 4, 2021, https://www.dailymaverick.co.za/article/2018-06-11-nelson-mandelas-leadership-his-obstinacy-and-commitment-to-freedom-part-2/.

4 Shirley Du Boulay, *Tutu: Voice of the Voiceless* (London: Hodder and Stoughton, 1988), 232.

5 Du Boulay, *Tutu*, 29.

6 "Desmond Tutu: Personal Life and Personality," *Wikipedia*, accessed October 12, 2021, https://en.wikipedia.org/wiki/Desmond_Tutu#Personal_life_and_personality.

7 "Desmond Tutu," *Wikipedia*, accessed October 12, 2021, https://en.wikipedia.org/wiki/Desmond_Tutu.

8 Desmond Tutu, "Truth and Reconciliation Commission, South Africa," Brittanica.com, accessed October 15, 2021, https://www.britannica.com/topic/Truth-and-Reconciliation-Commission-South-Africa.

9 Elaine N. Aron, *The Highly Sensitive Person: How to Thrive When the World Overwhelms You* (New York: Harmony, 2016), 150.

10 Barrie Jaeger, *Making Work Work for the Highly Sensitive Person: Learning to Bend, Not Break, When Work Overwhelms You* (New York: McGraw-Hill, 2004), 78–82.
11 Jaeger, *Making Work Work for the Highly Sensitive Person*, 82.
12 Henri J. M. Nouwen, Donald P. McNeil, and Douglas A. Morrison, *Compassion: A Reflection on the Christian Life* (New York: Image, 1983), 19.
13 Henry David Thoreau, "Civil Disobedience," American Studies at the University of Virginia, 1849, accessed February 23, 2022, https://xroads.virginia.edu/~Hyper2/thoreau/civil.html.
14 "Ubuntu Philosophy," *Wikipedia*, accessed February 10, 2022, https://en.wikipedia.org/wiki/Ubuntu_philosophy.

Chapter 6

1 Antonia Malchik, "The Problem with Social Media Protests," *Atlantic*, May 6, 2019, accessed February 1, 2022, https://www.theatlantic.com/technology/archive/2019/05/in-person-protests-stronger-online-activism-a-walking-life/578905/.
2 Indigenous Corporate Training Inc., "What Is the Seventh Generation Principle?" *Working Effectively with Indigenous Peoples Blog*, May 30, 2020, accessed February 1, 2022, https://www.ictinc.ca/blog/seventh-generation-principle.
3 "Khalida Brohi," *Wikipedia*, accessed February 23, 2022, https://en.wikipedia.org/wiki/Khalida_Brohi.
4 History.com editors, "Loving v. Virginia," History.com, November 17, 2017, updated January 25, 2021, updated February 12, 2022, https://www.history.com/topics/civil-rights-movement/loving-v-virginia.
5 Parker J. Palmer, *Let Your Life Speak: Listening for the Voice of Vocation* (San Francisco: Jossey-Bass, 2000), 2–3.
6 "Howard Thurman Quotes," Goodreads, accessed September 20, 2022, https://www.goodreads.com/quotes/582881-there-is-something-in-every-one-of-you-that-waits.

Chapter 7

1 Learning for Justice, "Juliette Hampton Morgan: A White Woman Who Understood," Learning for Justice, accessed November 16, 2021, https://www.learningforjustice.org/classroom-resources/lessons/juliette-hampton-morgan-a-white-woman-who-understood.
2 "Juliette Hampton Morgan," *Wikipedia*, accessed November 16, 2021, https://en.wikipedia.org/wiki/Juliette_Hampton_Morgan.
3 Barrie Jaeger, *Making Work Work for the Highly Sensitive Person: Learning to Bend, Not Break, When Work Overwhelms You* (New York: McGraw-Hill, 2004), 38.
4 Jaeger, *Making Work Work for the Highly Sensitive Person*, 36.
5 Paula Kamen, *Finding Iris Chang: Friendship, Ambition, and the Loss of an Extraordinary Mind* (Philadelphia: Da Capo Press, 2007), 5.

6 Margalit Fox, "Iris Chang, Who Chronicled Rape of Nanking, Dies at 36," *New York Times*, November 12, 2004, accessed December 8, 2021, https://www.nytimes.com/2004/11/12/arts/iris-chang-who-chronicled-rape-of-nanking-dies-at-36.html.

7 Orville Schell, "Bearing Witness," Books, *New York Times*, December 14, 1997, accessed December 8, 2021, https://archive.nytimes.com/www.nytimes.com/books/97/12/14/reviews/971214.14schellt.html?scp=17&sq=china%2520shame&st=cse.

8 "Iris Chang," *Wikipedia*, accessed December 8, 2021, https://en.wikipedia.org/wiki/Iris_Chang.

9 Rose Zimering and Suzy Bird Gulliver, "Secondary Traumatization in Mental Health Care Providers," *Psychiatric Times* 20, no. 4 (April 1, 2003), accessed December 10, 2021, https://www.psychiatrictimes.com/view/secondary-traumatization-mental-health-care-providers.

10 Zimering and Gulliver, "Secondary Traumatization in Mental Health Care Providers."

11 "Empathy Fatigue: How Stress and Trauma Can Take a Toll on You," Health Essentials, Cleveland Clinic, June 25, 2021, accessed December 10, 2021, https://health.clevelandclinic.org/empathy-fatigue-how-stress-and-trauma-can-take-a-toll-on-you/.

12 Andre Sólo, "The 7 Best Careers for a Highly Sensitive Person," *Highly Sensitive Refuge*, August 8, 2018, accessed January 14, 2022, https://highlysensitiverefuge.com/highly-sensitive-person-careers/.

13 Gil Bailie, *Violence Unveiled: Humanity at the Crossroads* (New York: Crossroad, 1997), xv.

Chapter 8

1 Mary E. Gomes, "The Rewards and Stresses of Social Change: A Qualitative Study of Peace Activists," *Journal of Humanistic Psychology* 32, no. 4 (Fall 1992), 141–43.

2 Nancy A. Hewitt, "Abolition and Suffrage," *Not for Ourselves Alone*, PBS, accessed December 10, 2021, https://www.pbs.org/kenburns/not-for-ourselves-alone/abolition-suffrage/.

3 Melissa Block, "Yes, Women Could Vote after the 19th Amendment—But Not All Women. Or Men," *Morning Edition*, NPR, August 26, 2020, accessed December 10, 2021, https://www.npr.org/2020/08/26/904730251/yes-women-could-vote-after-the-19th-amendment-but-not-all-women-or-men.

4 Sean Heather K. McGraw, *The Gay Liberation Movement: Before and after Stonewall* (New York: Rosen, 2019), 62–65.

5 Andrew Pulrang, "4 Important Things Disabled People Disagree About," *Forbes*, February 13, 2021, accessed December 10, 2021, https://www.forbes.com/sites/andrewpulrang/2021/02/13/4-important-things-disabled-people-disagree-about/?sh=5503c17a6f22.

6 Genevieve Graves, "Why People Quit Their Jobs," *Harvard Business Review*, September 2016, accessed December 11, 2021, https://hbr.org/2016/09/why-people-quit-their-jobs.

7 Gregg Ward, "Organizational Culture in the Age of Burnout: What Every Leader Should Know," *Forbes*, January 16, 2020, accessed December 11, 2021, https://www.forbes.com/sites/forbescoachescouncil/2020/01/16/organizational-culture-in-the-age-of-burnout-what-every-leader-should-know/?sh=3b2e99245b1b.

8 Marquetta Smith, "Top 12 Reasons Why Volunteers Quit," *Safe Harbor*, October 6, 2018, accessed December 11, 2021, https://safeharborim.com/top-reasons-why-volunteers-quit/.

9 Barrie Jaeger, *Making Work Work for the Highly Sensitive Person: Learning to Bend, Not Break, When Work Overwhelms You* (New York: McGraw-Hill, 2004), 39.

10 "Study: Most Nonprofits Lacking in Leadership, Management," *NonProfit Times*, November 1, 2017, accessed December 11, 2021, https://www.thenonprofittimes.com/npt_articles/study-nonprofits-lacking-leadership-management/.

11 Ali Akbar Bromideh, "The Widespread Challenges of NGOs in Developing Countries: Case Studies from Iran," *International NGO Journal* 6, no. 9 (September 2011), 199–200, accessed December 11, 2021, https://academicjournals.org/journal/INGOJ/article-full-text-pdf/117960141095.

12 Roger Bruns, *Cesar Chavez: A Biography* (Westport, CT: Greenwood, 2005), 98–99.

13 Bruns, *Cesar Chavez*, 100.

14 Shaazia Ebrahim, "Nelson Mandela and Women," *Daily Vox*, April 17, 2018, accessed December 13, 2021, https://www.thedailyvox.co.za/nelson-mandela-and-women-shaazia-ebrahim/.

15 "Bayard Rustin," *Wikipedia*, accessed September 1, 2021, accessed December 13, 2021, https://en.wikipedia.org/wiki/Bayard_Rustin. See also Michel Martin and Emma Bowman, "In Newly Forgotten Audio, a Forgotten Civil Rights Leader Says Coming Out 'Was an Absolute Necessity,'" *All Things Considered*, NPR, January 6, 2019, accessed December 13, 2021, https://www.npr.org/2019/01/06/682598649/in-newly-found-audio-a-forgotten-civil-rights-leader-says-coming-out-was-an-abso.

16 Tamoghna Halder, "Coming to Terms with Gandhi's Complicated Legacy," *Al Jazeera*, April 7, 2021, accessed December 13, 2021, https://www.aljazeera.com/opinions/2021/4/7/coming-to-terms-with-gandhis-complicated-legacy.

17 "Mahatma Gandhi," *Wikipedia*, accessed September 1, 2021, https://en.wikipedia.org/wiki/Mahatma_Gandhi.

18 "Emotional Labor," *Wikipedia*, accessed October 2, 2021, https://en.wikipedia.org/wiki/Emotional_labor.

19 Jaeger, *Making Work Work*, 86.

20 Melba Patillo Beals, *I Will Not Fear: My Story of a Lifetime of Building Faith under Fire* (Grand Rapids, MI: Revell, 2018), 27.

Chapter 9

1 Óscar Romero, *The Violence of Love*, comp. and trans. James R. Brockman, S.J. (Maryknoll, NY: Orbis, 1988), 2.
2 Sean Salai, "Interview: The Life and Martyrdom of Jesuit Rutilio Grande," *America: The Jesuit Review*, March 12, 2021, accessed December 3, 2021, https://www.americamagazine.org/arts-culture/2021/03/12/jesuit-rutilio-grande-salvador-martyr-biography-240210.
3 "Óscar Romero," *Wikipedia*, accessed December 3, 2021, https://en.wikipedia.org/wiki/%C3%93scar_Romero.
4 "Óscar Romero," *Wikipedia*.
5 History.com editors, "Vietnam War Protests," History.com, February 22, 2010, updated March 30, 2020, accessed December 9, 2021, https://www.history.com/topics/vietnam-war/vietnam-war-protests.
6 "Alicia Zubasnabar de De la Cuadra," *Wikipedia*, accessed July 19, 2022, https://en.wikipedia.org/wiki/Alicia_Zubasnabar_de_De_la_Cuadra.
7 Elaine N. Aron, *The Highly Sensitive Parent: Be Brilliant in Your Role, Even When the World Overwhelms You* (New York: Kensington, 2020), 2–5.
8 The Editors of Encyclopedia Britannica, "St. Óscar Romero," Britannica.com, accessed December 7, 2021, https://www.britannica.com/biography/Oscar-Arnulfo-Romero.
9 The Editors of Encyclopedia Britannica, updated by Erik Gregerson, "Dorothea Dix," Britannica.com, accessed December 7, 2021, https://www.britannica.com/biography/Dorothea-Dix.
10 Yuki Ueno, Aki Takahashi, and Atsushi Oshio, "Relationship between Sensory-Processing Sensitivity and Age in a Large Cross-Sectional Japanese Sample," *Heliyon* 5, no. 10 (October 2019), accessed December 13, 2021, https://www.ncbi.nlm.nih.gov/pmc/articles/PMC6812185/.
11 McLean Hospital, "How Emotional Sensitivity Changes as We Age," *Technology Networks*, March 4, 2019, accessed December 13, 2021, https://www.technologynetworks.com/neuroscience/news/how-emotional-sensitivity-changes-as-we-age-316240.
12 "Sensitivity to Noise as We Age," Pacific Northwest Audiology, accessed December 13, 2021, https://pnwaudiology.com/blog/sensitivity-to-noise-as-we-age/. See also "Aging Changes in the Senses," Medline Plus, accessed December 13, 2021, https://medlineplus.gov/ency/article/004013.htm.

Chapter 10

1 Seema Rajpal, "The Bill Drayton Interview: The Story behind How the Ashoka Fellowship Was Created after a Roadtrip to India," *Edex Live*, January 19, 2021, accessed February 2, 2022, https://www.edexlive.com/happening/2021/jan/19/the-bill-drayton-interview-the-story-behind-how-the-ashoka-fellowship-was-created-after-a-roadtrip-17384.html.

2 "Ashoka in the United States," Ashoka, accessed February 2, 2022, https://www.ashoka.org/en-us/country/united-states.

3 European Commission, "The Social Business Initiative of the European Commission," n.d., accessed February 3, 2022, https://ec.europa.eu/docsroom/documents/14583/attachments/3/translations/en/renditions/native.

4 Josh Bersin, "The Rise of the Social Enterprise: A New Paradigm for Business," *Forbes*, April 3, 2018, accessed February 3, 2022, https://www.forbes.com/sites/joshbersin/2018/04/03/the-rise-of-the-social-enterprise-a-new-paradigm-for-business/?sh=1a0a8ac171f0.

5 Julia Carmel, "'Nothing about Us without Us': 16 Moments in the Fight for Disability Rights," *New York Times*, July 22, 2020, updated July 29, 2020, accessed December 8, 2021, https://www.nytimes.com/2020/07/22/us/ada-disabilities-act-history.html.

6 Barrie Jaeger, *Making Work Work for the Highly Sensitive Person: Learning to Bend, Not Break, When Work Overwhelms You* (New York: McGraw-Hill, 2004), 44.

7 Denise Lee Yohn, "Company Culture Is Everyone's Responsibility," *Harvard Business Review*, February 8, 2021, accessed January 14, 2022, https://hbr.org/2021/02/company-culture-is-everyones-responsibility.

8 Yohn, "Company Culture Is Everyone's Responsibility."

9 Roger Bruns, *Cesar Chavez: A Biography* (Westport, CT: Greenwood, 2005), 92.

10 David Van Biema, "Mother Teresa's Crisis of Faith," *TIME*, August 23, 2007, accessed November 6, 2021, https://time.com/4126238/mother-teresas-crisis-of-faith/.

Chapter 11

1 Tom Vanderbilt, "The Psychology of Genre," *New York Times*, May 28, 2016, accessed November 7, 2021, https://www.nytimes.com/2016/05/29/opinion/sunday/the-psychology-of-genre.html.

2 Rachael Rettner, "Not Your Imagination: Kids Today Really Are Less Creative," *Today*, August 12, 2011, accessed November 14, 2021, https://www.today.com/parents/not-your-imagination-kids-today-really-are-less-creative-study-wbna44122383.

3 Lara Logan, "How Unconventional Thinking Transformed a War-Torn Colombia," *60 Minutes*, CBS News, December 11, 2016, accessed January 29, 2022, https://www.cbsnews.com/news/60-minutes-colombia-after-civil-war-lara-logan/.

4 "Colombia," *Wikipedia*, accessed January 29, 2022, https://en.wikipedia.org/wiki/Colombia.

5 Bill Burnett and Dave Evans, *Designing Your Life: Build the Perfect Career, Step by Step* (London: Vintage, 2018), 38.

6 Izzeldin Abuelaish, *I Shall Not Hate: A Gaza Doctor's Journey on the Road to Peace and Human Dignity* (New York: Walker & Co., 2010), 135.

7 Parker J. Palmer, *Let Your Life Speak: Listening for the Voice of Vocation* (San Francisco: Wiley, 2000), 2–3.

Chapter 12

1 "Definitions of Social Capital," Institute for Social Capital, accessed September 14, 2022, https://www.socialcapitalresearch.com/literature/definition/.

2 Paul S. Adler and Seok-Woo Kwon, "Social Capital: Prospects for a New Concept," *Academy of Management Review* 27, no. 1 (2002), 17–40.

3 Robert D. Putnam, *Bowling Alone: The Collapse and Revival of American Community* (New York: Simon & Schuster, 2001), 15–20.

4 Elena Renken, "Most Americans Are Lonely, and Our Workplace Culture May Not Be Helping," NPR, January 20, 2020, accessed October 12, 2021, https://www.npr.org/sections/health-shots/2020/01/23/798676465/most-americans-are-lonely-and-our-workplace-culture-may-not-be-helping.

5 Lee Raine, Scott Keeter, and Andrew Perrin, "Trust and Distrust in America," Pew Research Center, July 22, 2019, accessed October 12, 2021, https://www.pewresearch.org/politics/2019/07/22/trust-and-distrust-in-america/.

6 Putnam, *Bowling Alone*, 35–36.

7 Tristan Claridge, "What Is Bonding Social Capital?" Social Capital Research, January 6, 2018, accessed October 12, 2021, https://www.socialcapitalresearch.com/what-is-bonding-social-capital/.

8 Claridge, "What Is Bonding Social Capital?"

9 Doug McAdam and Ronnelle Paulsen, "Specifying the Relationship between Social Ties and Activism," *American Journal of Sociology* 99, no. 3 (November 1993), 640–67.

10 Bruce Watson, adapted by Rebecca Stefoff, *Freedom Summer: The Violent Season that Made Mississippi Burn and Made America a Democracy (for Young People)* (New York: Seven Stories, 2020), 89.

11 Watson, *Freedom Summer*, 154–55.

12 History.com editors, "Freedom Summer," History.com, October 29, 2009, updated April 16, 2021, accessed October 14, 2021, https://www.history.com/topics/black-history/freedom-summer.

13 "PTSD, Freedom Summer, 1964," Mississippi Public Broadcasting, updated July 28, 2014, accessed October 14, 2021, https://www.youtube.com/watch?v=XsZmy3QIVi8.

14 Sara O'Shaughnessy and Emily Huddart Kennedy, "Relational Activism: Reimagining Women's Environmental Work as Cultural Change," *Canadian Journal of Sociology* 35, no. 4 (December 29, 2010), 551–72.

15 O'Shaughnessy and Kennedy, "Relational Activism," 552–53.

16 Becca Dove and Tim Fisher, "Becoming Unstuck with Relational Activism," *Stanford Social Innovation Review*, October 10, 2019, accessed October 6, 2021, https://ssir.org/articles/entry/becoming_unstuck_with_relational_activism.

17 "Daryl Davis," *Wikipedia*, accessed October 6, 2021, https://en.wikipedia.org/wiki/Daryl_Davis.
18 Nicholas Kristof, "How Can You Hate Me When You Don't Even Know Me?" *New York Times*, June 26, 2021, accessed October 6, 2021, https://www.nytimes.com/2021/06/26/opinion/racism-politics-daryl-davis.html.
19 "The Better Conversations Guide," OnBeing.org, accessed October 7, 2021, https://onbeing.org/civil-conversations-project/better-conversations-guide/.
20 Kristoff, "How Can You Hate Me."
21 Dove and Fisher, "Becoming Unstuck."
22 Dove and Fisher, "Becoming Unstuck."
23 "A Mile in My Shoes," Empathy Museum, accessed February 18, 2022, https://www.empathymuseum.com/a-mile-in-my-shoes/.

Chapter 13

1 Jacques E. Levy, *Cesar Chavez: Autobiography of La Causa* (Minneapolis: University of Minnesota, 2007), 198.
2 "El Teatro Campesino: Organizational History," UC Santa Barbara Library, accessed November 17, 2021, https://www.library.ucsb.edu/special-collections/cema/etc.
3 "El Teatro Campesino."
4 "El Teatro Campesino," *Wikipedia*, accessed November 17, 2021, https://en.wikipedia.org/wiki/El_Teatro_Campesino.
5 Jorge J. Huerta, "El Teatro's Living Legacy," *American Theatre*, November 21, 2016, accessed November 17, 2021, https://www.americantheatre.org/2016/11/21/el-teatros-living-legacy.
6 Kimberly L. Kontson, Murad Megjhani, Justin A. Brantley, Jesus G. Cruz-Garza, Sho Nakagome, Dario Robleto, Michelle White, Eugene Civillico, and Jose L. Contreras-Vidal, "Your Brain on Art: Emergent Cortical Dynamics During Aesthetic Experiences," *Frontiers in Human Neuroscience* 9, no. 18 (November 2015), accessed November 29, 2021, https://www.frontiersin.org/articles/10.3389/fnhum.2015.00626/full.
7 Susan Magsamen, "Your Brain on Art: The Case for Neuroaesthetics," *Cerebrum*, July 1, 2019, accessed November 22, 2021, https://www.ncbi.nlm.nih.gov/pmc/articles/PMC7075503/.
8 Megan Schmidt, "How Reading Fiction Increases Empathy and Encourages Understanding," *Discover*, August 28, 2020, accessed November 22, 2021, https://www.discovermagazine.com/mind/how-reading-fiction-increases-empathy-and-encourages-understanding.
9 "What Did We Achieve at the Marks and Spencer AGM for Shareholders?" Craftivist Collective, July 8, accessed November 17, 2021, https://craftivist-collective.com/What-we-achieved-at-Marks-and-Spencer-AGM.
10 Ron Eyerman, "The Art of Social Movement," in *The Oxford Handbook of Social Movements*, ed. Donatella Della Porta and Mario Diani (Oxford: Oxford

University Press, 2015), accessed December 2, 2021, https://www.oxfordhandbooks.com/view/10.1093/oxfordhb/9780199678402.001.0001/oxfordhb-9780199678402-e-47.

11 Nicolas Lampert, *A People's Art History of the United States: 250 Years of Activist Art and Artists Working in Social Justice Movements* (New York: New Press, 2013), 1–10.

12 Lampert, *A People's Art History*, 24–27.

13 K. K. Ottesen, *Activist: Portraits of Courage* (Auckland: Chronicle Books, 2019), 19.

14 Elaine N. Aron, *The Highly Sensitive Person: How to Thrive When the World Overwhelms You* (New York: Harmony, 2016), 124.

15 "Pearl S. Buck Quotes," Goodreads, accessed November 19, 2021, https://www.goodreads.com/quotes/31946-the-truly-creative-mind-in-any-field-is-no-more.

16 Lampert, *People's Art History*, xi.

17 Kontson et al., "Your Brain on Art."

18 Stephen Hicks, "Plato on Censoring Artists—A Summary," Stephen Hicks, PhD, Philosopher blog, accessed November 23, 2021, http://www.stephenhicks.org/2012/01/21/plato-on-censoring-artists-a-summary/.

19 "Ai Weiwei," *Wikipedia*, accessed November 23, 2021, https://en.wikipedia.org/wiki/Ai_Weiwei.

20 Ishaan Tharoor, "A Jailed Iranian Musician Texts from His Hospital Bed: Don't Forget Me," *Washington Post*, December 2, 2016, accessed November 23, 2021, https://www.washingtonpost.com/news/worldviews/wp/2016/12/02/a-jailed-iranian-musician-texts-from-his-hospital-bed-dont-forget-me/.

21 "Imprisoned Artists," Voice Project, accessed November 23, 2021, http://voiceproject.org/campaign/imprisoned-artists/.

22 Taylor Dafoe, "Dissenting Artists around the Globe Were Jailed and Killed at an Alarming Rate Last Year, According to a New Report," Artnet.com, March 3, 2021, accessed November 23, 2021, https://news.artnet.com/art-world/state-of-artistic-freedom-2021-report-1948565.

23 Sarah Corbett, *How to Be a Craftivist: The Art of Gentle Protest* (London: Unbound, 2017), 2.

24 Megan Elizabeth Morrissey, "How Art Installations on the US-Mexico Border Affected People's Understanding of the Border," trans. Mary Grace Hébert, *Communication Currents*, National Communication Association, June 30, 2020, accessed November 24, 2021, https://www.natcom.org/communication-currents/how-art-installations-us-mexico-border-affected-peoples-understanding-border.

25 Wallace Ludel, "Seesaw Installations at US-Mexico Border Wins Design of the Year Award," *Art Newspaper*, January 20, 2021, accessed November 24, 2021, https://www.theartnewspaper.com/2021/01/20/seesaw-installation-at-us-mexico-border-wins-design-of-the-year-award.

Chapter 14

1 Diane D. Turner, "William Still's National Significance," Temple University Libraries, accessed December 15, 2021, http://stillfamily.library.temple.edu/exhibits/show/william-still/historical-perspective/william-still---s-national-sig.

2 "William Still," *Wikipedia*, accessed December 15, 2021, https://en.wikipedia.org/wiki/William_Still.

3 Valerie Russ, "William Still at 200: Philadelphia Will Honor the Abolitionist Whose Journal Told Underground Railroad Stories," *Philadelphia Inquirer*, October 6, 2021, accessed December 15, 2021, https://www.inquirer.com/news/william-still-200-anniversary-journal-underground-railroad-display-20211005.html.

4 "Underground Railroad: The William Still Story," PBS, accessed December 15, 2021, http://www.pbs.org/black-culture/shows/list/underground-railroad/home/.

5 "William Still," *Wikipedia*.

6 Randall C. Jimerson, *Archives Power: Memory, Accountability, and Social Justice* (Chicago: Society of American Archivists, 2009).

7 Jimerson, *Archives Power*.

8 Andrew Flinn, David A. Wallace, Renée Saucier, and Wendy M. Duff, eds., *Archives, Recordkeeping, and Social Justice* (London: Taylor & Francis, 2020), 2.

9 Flinn et al., *Archives, Recordkeeping, and Social Justice*, 2–3.

10 Brad Evans and Henry A. Giroux, "The Violence of Forgetting," *New York Times*, June 20, 2016, accessed January 15, 2022, https://www.nytimes.com/2016/06/20/opinion/the-violence-of-forgetting.html.

11 Sally Gimson, "Who Controls the Past Controls the Future…" *Index on Censorship* 47, no. 1, accessed January 15, 2022, https://journals.sagepub.com/doi/pdf/10.1177/0306422018770095.

12 "Peter Bryce," *Wikipedia*, accessed January 17, 2022, https://en.wikipedia.org/wiki/Peter_Bryce.

13 "Until There Is Not a Single Indian in Canada," Facing History and Ourselves, an excerpt from *Stolen Lives: The Indigenous Peoples of Canada and the Indian Residential Programs*, accessed January 17, 2022, https://www.facinghistory.org/stolen-lives-indigenous-peoples-canada-and-indian-residential-schools/historical-background/until-there-not-single-indian-canada.

14 International Council on Archives, "Basic Principles on the Role of Archivists and Records Managers in Support of Human Rights," September 2016, 2, accessed January 23, 2022, https://www.ica.org/en/basic-principles-on-the-role-of-archivists-and-records-managers-in-support-of-human-rights-0.

15 Gary A. Haugen, *Good News about Injustice* (Downers Grove, IL: InterVarsity, 1999), 29.

16 United Nations, "UN Tribunal on Rwandan Genocide Formally Closes—Major Role in Fight against Impunity," *UN News*, December 31, 2015, accessed

February 3, 2022, https://news.un.org/en/story/2015/12/519212-un-tribunal-rwandan-genocide-formally-closes-major-role-fight-against-impunity.

17 E. Ndenje-Sichalwe and P. Ngulube, "Records Management and Access to Information: Key to Fostering Accountability, Good Governance, and Protection of Human Rights in Tanzania," *Journal of the Eastern and Southern Africa Regional Branch of the International Council on Archives* 28 (2009), accessed January 23, 2022, https://www.ajol.info/index.php/esarjo/article/view/44394.

18 Elisabeth Baumgartner, Brandon Hamber, Briony Jones, Gráinne Kelly, and Ingrid Oliveira, "Documentation, Human Rights and Transitional Justice," *Journal of Human Rights Practice* 8, no. 1 (February 2016), 1–5, accessed January 23, 2022, https://doi.org/10.1093/jhuman/huw002.

19 International Council on Archives, "Basic Principles on the Role of Archivists and Records Managers," 3.

20 International Council on Archives, "Basic Principles on the Role of Archivists and Records Managers," 3.

21 "The Role of Empathy in Health and Social Care Professionals," *Healthcare (Basel)* 8, no. 1 (March 2020), 26, accessed January 8, 2022, https://www.ncbi.nlm.nih.gov/pmc/articles/PMC7151200/.

22 Meredith Deliso, "Darnella Frazier, Who Recorded Video of George Floyd's Death, Recognized by Pulitzer Board," ABC News, June 11, 2021, accessed June 22, 2022, https://abcnews.go.com/US/darnella-frazier-recognized-pulitzer-prizes-george-floyd-video/story?id=78225202.

23 Linly Lin, "Cynthia Choi, Russell Jeung, & Manjusha Kulkarni, AAPI Protectors," Bloomberg.com, December 1, 2021, accessed January 28, 2022, https://www.bloomberg.com/news/articles/2021-12-01/stop-aapi-hate-data-fights-racism-during-covid-crisis-bloomberg-50-2021.

24 Latasha Morrison, *Be the Bridge: Pursuing God's Heart for Racial Reconciliation* (Colorado Springs: WaterBrook, 2019), 2.

Chapter 15

1 History.com editors, "Printing Press," History.com, May 7, 2018, updated October 10, 2019, accessed December 9, 2021, https://www.history.com/topics/inventions/printing-press.

2 Dave Roos, "7 Ways the Printing Press Changed the World," History.com, August 28, 2019, updated September 3, 2019, accessed December 9, 2021, https://www.history.com/news/printing-press-renaissance.

3 "Scribe," *Wikipedia*, accessed December 21, 2021, https://en.wikipedia.org/wiki/Scribe.

4 Elizabeth L. Eistenstein, *The Printing Press as an Agent of Change: Communications and Cultural Transformations in Early-Modern Europe*, vol. 1 and 2 (Cambridge: Cambridge University Press, 1979), 3.

5 Roos, "7 Ways the Printing Press Changed the World."

6 Chelsea Greenwood, "9 Subtle Ways Technology Is Making Humanity Worse," *Business Insider*, August 23, 2019, accessed December 22, 2021, https://www.businessinsider.com/technology-negative-bad-effects-society-2019-8.

7 "Technology," *Merriam-Webster Online Dictionary*, accessed December 21, 2021, https://www.merriam-webster.com/dictionary/technology.

8 Joseph Shapiro, "Re-inventing the Wheel," Alicia Patterson Foundation, April 15, 2011, accessed December 18, 2021, https://aliciapatterson.org/stories/re-inventing-wheel.

9 "More People Have Access to Energy than Ever Before, but World Is Falling Short of Sustainable Energy Goals," World Health Organization, May 21, 2019, accessed December 20, 2021, https://www.who.int/news/item/21-05-2019-more-people-have-access-to-electricity-than-ever-before-but-world-is-falling-short-of-sustainable-energy-goals.

10 "Transport: Overview," World Bank, last updated June 30, 2021, accessed December 20, 2021, https://www.worldbank.org/en/topic/transport/overview.

11 Alex Gailey and Kendall Little, "What You Should Know If You Are Unbanked Right Now," *TIME*, June 4, 2021, accessed December 20, 2021, https://time.com/nextadvisor/banking/what-to-know-if-you-are-unbanked/.

12 "Two-Thirds of World's School-Age Children Have No Internet Access at Home, New UNICEF-ITU Report Says," UNICEF, November 30, 2020, accessed December 20, 2021, https://www.unicef.org/press-releases/two-thirds-worlds-school-age-children-have-no-internet-access-home-new-unicef-itu.

13 UNESCO Global Education Monitoring Report Team, "Accountability in Education: Meeting Our Commitments, Global Education Monitoring Report, 2017–18," UNESCO, accessed December 20, 2021, https://unesdoc.unesco.org/ark:/48223/pf0000259338.

14 Susan B. Neuman and Naomi Moland, "Book Deserts: The Consequences of Income Segregation on Children's Access to Print," *Urban Education* 54, no. 1 (July 5, 2016), 126–47.

15 "*Nia Teen* Magazine," ZanaAfrica Foundation, accessed September 12, 2022, http://www.zanaafrica.org/health-education-2/.

16 Bill Been, "Design for the Other 90%," *Fast Company*, May 10, 2007, accessed August 9, 2021, https://www.fastcompany.com/678764/design-other-90.

17 Paul Polak, *Out of Poverty: What Works When Traditional Approaches Fail* (San Francisco: Berrett-Koehler, 2008), 1.

18 Rikke Friis Dam and Teo Yu Siang, "Design Thinking: A Quick Overview," Interaction Design Foundation, 2020, accessed August 9, 2021, https://www.interaction-design.org/literature/article/design-thinking-a-quick-overview?nam_source=https%3A%2F%2Fnotamagazine.xyz.

19 Tim Brown and Jocelyn Wyatt, "Design Thinking for Social Innovation," *Stanford Social Innovation Review*, Winter 2010, accessed August 9, 2021, https://ssir.org/articles/entry/design_thinking_for_social_innovation.

20 Associated Press, "Examples of Failed Aid-Funded Projects in Africa," NBC, December 23, 2007, https://www.nbcnews.com/id/wbna22380448.

21 "Failure in International Aid," GiveWell, accessed August 9, 2021, https://www.givewell.org/international/technical/criteria/impact/failure-stories#Poorly_executed_programs.

22 Jeffrey Gettleman, "Meant to Keep Malaria Out, Mosquito Nets Are Used to Haul Fish In," *New York Times*, January 24, 2015, accessed August 9, 2021, https://www.nytimes.com/2015/01/25/world/africa/mosquito-nets-for-malaria-spawn-new-epidemic-overfishing.html.

23 Simon K. Andersson-Manjang and Nika Naghavi, "State of the Industry Report on Mobile Money 2021," GSM Association, accessed August 11, 2021, https://www.gsma.com/mobilefordevelopment/wp-content/uploads/2021/03/GSMA_State-of-the-Industry-Report-on-Mobile-Money-2021_Full-report.pdf.

Chapter 16

1 "Rosa Parks," *Wikipedia*, accessed September 8, 2021, https://en.wikipedia.org/wiki/Rosa_Parks.

2 "Highlander Folk School," SNCC Digital Gateway, accessed September 8, 2021, https://snccdigital.org/inside-sncc/alliances-relationships/highlander/.

3 Sheila Hardy and P. Stephen Hardy, *Extraordinary People of the Civil Rights Movement* (New York: Children's Press, 2007), 49.

4 Hardy and Hardy, *Extraordinary People of the Civil Rights Movement*, 49.

5 Myles Horton, Judith Kohl, and Herbert Kohl, *The Long Haul: An Autobiography* (New York: Teachers College Press, 1997), 127.

6 "88 Years of Fighting for Justice," Highlander Research and Education Center, accessed September 9, 2021, https://highlandercenter.org/our-history-timeline.

7 "When Elizabeth Cady Stanton Met Lucretia Mott, the Women's Movement Began (Supposedly)," New England Historical Society, accessed January 7, 2022, https://www.newenglandhistoricalsociety.com/when-elizabeth-cady-stanton-met-lucretia-mott-the-womens-movement-began/.

8 Lori D. Ginzberg, *Elizabeth Cady Stanton: An American Life* (New York: Hill and Wang, 2009), 39.

9 Debra Michels, ed., "Elizabeth Cady Stanton," National Women's History Museum, 2017, accessed January 7, 2022, https://www.womenshistory.org/education-resources/biographies/elizabeth-cady-stanton.

10 "Susan B. Anthony," *Wikipedia*, accessed February 19, 2022, https://en.wikipedia.org/wiki/Susan_B._Anthony.

11 Judith E. Harper, "Biography," *Not for Ourselves Alone*, PBS, accessed February 19, 2022, https://www.pbs.org/kenburns/not-for-ourselves-alone/biography/.

12 Eli A. Wolff and Dr. Mary Hums, "Power of Mentoring for Social Change," *HuffPost*, July 17, 2015, updated July 17, 2016, accessed January 24, 2022, https://www.huffpost.com/entry/power-of-mentoring-for-so_b_7810664.

13 Teresa Tillman, "The Good and Bad of Sensitivity in Teachers," SensitivityResearch.com, May 9, 2020, accessed November 17, 2021, https://sensitivityresearch.com/the-good-and-bad-of-sensitivity-in-teachers/.

14 Julie Stefan Lindsay, "The Highly Sensitive Teacher: Sensory-Processing Sensitivity, Burnout, and Self-Efficacy in Urban Public School Teachers" (diss., University of California Los Angeles, 2017), ProQuest, November 17, 2021, https://www.proquest.com/openview/0d8525087ec223b8eb760032dbd7ca71/1?pq-origsite=gscholar&cbl=18750&diss=y.

15 Abigail Johnson Hess, "LinkedIn: 94% of Employees Say They Would Stay at a Company Longer for This One Reason—And It's Not a Raise," CNBC, February 27, 2019, accessed September 16, 2021, https://www.cnbc.com/2019/02/27/94percent-of-employees-would-stay-at-a-company-for-this-one-reason.html.

16 Jena McGregor, "To Improve Diversity, Don't Make People Go to Diversity Trainings. Really," *Washington Post*, July 1, 2016, accessed December 3, 2021, https://www.washingtonpost.com/news/on-leadership/wp/2016/07/01/to-improve-diversity-dont-make-people-go-to-diversity-training-really-2/.

17 "Ironic Effects of Anti-Prejudice Messages," Association for Psychological Research, July 6, 2011, accessed December 3, 2021, http://www.psychologicalscience.org/news/releases/ironic-effects-of-anti-prejudice-messages.html.

18 Poppy Noor, "So Your Company Uses Diversity Training. Does It Even Work?" *The Guardian*, March 10, 2021, accessed December 6, 2021, https://www.theguardian.com/world/2021/mar/10/workplace-diversity-training-does-it-work-racial-justice.

19 Sal Meyers, Katherine Rowell, Mary Wells, and Brian C. Smith, "Teacher Empathy: A Model of Empathy for Teaching for Student Success," *College Teaching* 67, no. 3 (April 2019), 160, accessed December 3, 2021, https://www.tandfonline.com/doi/abs/10.1080/87567555.2019.1579699?journalCode=vcol20.

20 Conor Friedersdorf, "Can Chloé Valdary Sell Skeptics on DEI?" *Atlantic*, January 31, 2021, accessed December 3, 2021, https://www.theatlantic.com/ideas/archive/2021/01/can-chloe-valdary-sell-skeptics-dei/617875/.

Chapter 17

1 Erin Blakemore, "How Dolls Helped Win Brown v. Board of Education," History.com, March 27, 2018, updated January 11, 2022, accessed

February 20, 2022, https://www.history.com/news/brown-v-board-of-education-doll-experiment.

2 Blakemore, "How Dolls Helped Win Brown v. Board of Education."

3 "A Revealing Experiment: Brown v. Board and 'The Doll Test,'" NAACP Legal Defense Fund, accessed February 20, 2022, https://www.naacpldf.org/ldf-celebrates-60th-anniversary-brown-v-board-education/significance-doll-test/.

4 "A Revealing Experiment."

5 Blakemore, "How Dolls Helped Win Brown v. Board of Education."

6 Heather Z. Lyons, Denise H. Bike, Lizette Ojeda, Adanna Johnson, Rocío Rosales, and Lisa Y. Flores, "Qualitative Research as a Social Justice Practice with Culturally Diverse Populations," *Journal for Social Action in Counseling and Psychology* 5, no. 2 (2013), 11, accessed February 20, 2022, https://openjournals.bsu.edu/jsacp/article/view/485/463.

7 Sarah Baughey-Gill, "When Gay Was Not Okay with the APA: A Historical Overview of Homosexuality and Its Status as Mental Disorder," *Occam's Razor* 1, article 2 (2011), 10–11, accessed February 6, 2022, https://cedar.wwu.edu/orwwu/vol1/iss1/2.

8 National Science Foundation, "Survey of Earned Doctorates 2019," accessed January 30, 2022, https://ncses.nsf.gov/pubs/nsf21308/data-tables; World Economic Forum, "Which Countries Have the Most Doctoral Candidates?" October 15, 2019, accessed January 30, 2022, https://www.weforum.org/agenda/2019/10/doctoral-graduates-phd-tertiary-education/.

9 Andrea Baertl, "2019 Think Tank State of the Sector Report," On Think Tanks, November 2020, accessed January 30, 2022, https://onthinktanks.org/publications/2019-think-tank-state-of-the-sector/.

10 Asit K. Biswas and Julian Kirchherr, "Prof, No One Is Reading You," *Straits Times*, April 11, 2015, accessed January 31, 2022, https://www.straitstimes.com/opinion/prof-no-one-is-reading-you.

11 Warren E. Leary, "Gun in Home? Study Finds It a Dangerous Mix," *New York Times*, October 7, 1993, Section A, page 18, accessed January 21, 2022, https://www.nytimes.com/1993/10/07/us/gun-in-home-study-finds-it-a-deadly-mix.html.

12 Sheryl Gay Stolberg, "Can New Gun Violence Research Find a Path around the Political Stalemate?" *New York Times*, March 27, 2021, accessed January 21, 2022, https://www.nytimes.com/2021/03/27/us/politics/gun-violence-research-cdc.html.

13 Save Heleta, "Academics Can Change the World—If They Stop Talking Only to Their Peers," *The Conversation*, March 8, 2016, updated March 31, 2017, accessed December 24, 2021, https://theconversation.com/academics-can-change-the-world-if-they-stop-talking-only-to-their-peers-55713.

14 "Robert D. Bullard," *Wikipedia*, accessed December 25, 2021, https://en.wikipedia.org/wiki/Robert_D._Bullard.

15 Renee Skelton and Vernice Miller, "The Environmental Justice Movement," National Resources Defense Council, March 17, 2016, accessed December 25, 2021, https://www.nrdc.org/stories/environmental-justice-movement.

16 Stephen H. Schneider, *Science as a Contact Sport: Inside the Battle to Save Earth's Climate* (Washington, DC: National Geographic Society, 2009), 15.

17 Louis Bergeron and Dan Stober, "Stephen Schneider, a Leading Climate Expert, Dead at 65," *Stanford Report*, July 19, 2010, accessed December 21, 2021, https://news.stanford.edu/news/2010/july/schneider-071910.html.

Chapter 18

1 Parker J. Palmer, *Let Your Life Speak: Listening for the Voice of Vocation* (San Francisco: Wiley, 2000), 2–3.

2 Austin Channing Brown, *I'm Still Here: Black Dignity in a World Made for Whiteness* (New York: Convergent, 2018), 180.

3 Daisaku Ikeda, *Hope Is a Decision: Selected Essays* (Santa Monica, CA: Middleway Pres, 2017), 2.

Appendix

1 Elaine N. Aron, *The Highly Sensitive Person: How to Thrive When the World Overwhelms You* (New York: Harmony, 2016), 29.

2 Aron, *The Highly Sensitive Person*, 30.

3 Christine Rose Elle, *The Happy Empath: A Survival Guide for Highly Sensitive People* (Emeryville, CA: Rockridge, 2019), 7–10. Used with the kind permission of Christine Rose Elle.